Dear Mr. Munari,

I like your book abou the zoo. My momma's wri this for me. I'm five. 5

You forgot to put any butterflies on the polar bear page.

Love,

TAMMY
AYYOUB

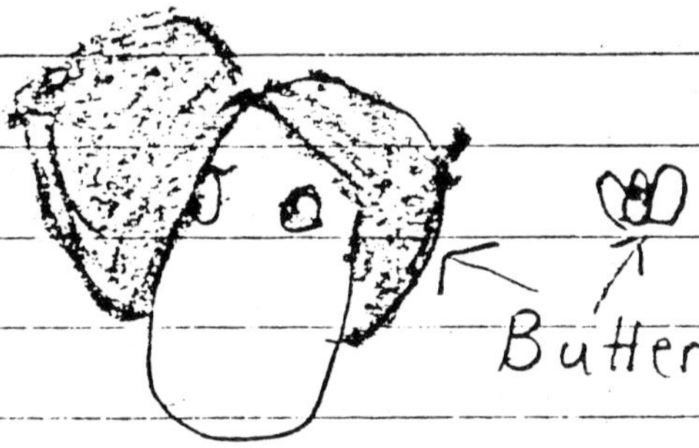

Butterflies

Bettagene
Grea

ary

Duane Pike

Ross
Gwendolyn
Ruberr
Debbi Ann
Freddy

Clarence
Pamela
Mary

Debbie Your
Lee

舞

How do you make the pictures?

Ronald
Charlotte
Brenda
Aline   Timothy
John B
Rhonda
Sandy
Deborah. Lyn

Eleonora

Aldo Tanchis

BRUNO MUNARI

ブルーノ・ムナーリ

MUNARI

Bruno Munari

ברונו מונארי

Brunom Munarijem

мунари

Design as Art

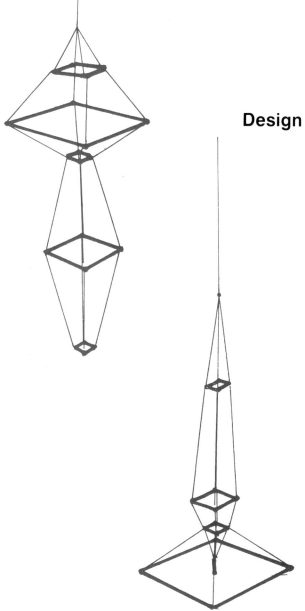

'To keep the spirit of childhood
within oneself for the whole of one's life
means retaining
the curiosity of knowing
the pleasure of understanding
the desire to communicate'

The MIT Press
Cambridge, Massachusetts

Editorial conception: Passigli Progetti
Art Direction: Bruno Munari
Translated from the Italian by Huw Evans

Photographic references

Ada Ardessi, Aldo Ballo, Gianni Berengo Gardin,
Clarifoto, Cesare Colombo, De Biasi, Angelo Furia,
Giorgio Furla, Ugo Mulas, Patellani, Petraroli,
Montecatini Photographic Agency.

First MIT Press English language edition, 1987
© 1986 Idea Books Edizioni. Originally published
in Italian as *Bruno Munari*, by Idea Books Edizioni,
Milan, Italy.

This book was set, printed and bound in Italy.

Contents

3 Preface by Andrea Branzi
6 From childhood to the 1930s
28 Graphics, theatre, painting, writing and other
   activities
52 Art as profession
94 Towards an art for everyone
138 Notes
139 Bibliography
142 Chronology of works
143 Exhibitions by Bruno Munari

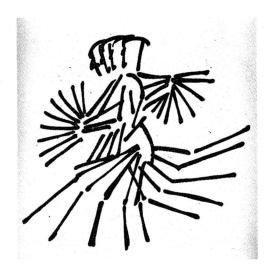

Pencil on paper, 1932.

Library of Congress Cataloging-in-Publication Data
Tanchis, Aldo, 1955-
   Bruno Munari: design as art.

   Translation of: Bruno Munari.
   Bibliography: p. 139.
   1. Munari, Bruno—Criticism and interpretation.
2. Design—Italy—History—20th century. I. Munari,
Bruno. II. Title.
NK1535.M86T3613 1987   709'.2'4   87-15272
ISBN 0-262-20065-1

Preface

We are often asked, and often ask ourselves, in what does the spirit of Italian design really consist? Where does it come from, this design which is apparently so unique that it is scrutinised with great curiosity by manufacturers and designers from all over the world?

It is my view that the spirit and identity of Italian design arise out of a fairly unusual set of historical factors. They are all factors that in a curious fashion combined to create a situation that was actually unfavourable to the development of classic design in Italy, but which have been turned on their head to become a different sort of design synergy, one that is certainly fragile but which has great creative vitality. They have served as an excellent cultural medium for an atypical system of design, of broad international consequence, but whose mode of operation would certainly not have been feasible anywhere else in the world.

If I were obliged to sum up these historical and environmental influences in a very concise way, I would point to three major considerations. The first of these is represented by the history of modern design in Italy. In spite of numerous historical falsehoods in circulation, Italian design was in no way born out of international rationalism. Indeed, there has never been any kind of rationalist movement in Italy, either before or after the war. The history of modern culture in Italy is characterised by the recurrent appearance of two great historical categories, Futurism and the Novecento. Only on the narrow boundary that separates these two areas can be found the masters of so-called Italian rationality. On close examination, however, it is apparent that even they have always been subject to the influence (a heretical one with respect to rationalist orthodoxy) of these two great tendencies. This is true of Gardella and Albini, as well as of Baldessari and Giò Ponti.

Even Fascism established its widespread popularity among the intellectuals of the design world by acting as an ambiguous intermediary between the two categories: revolution as historical continuity, modernity as national identity. And Italian design retained much of its Futurist stamp, in the notion of a technology that produces not certainties but continual transformations, the sign as dynamic vector and the method as never-ending research: like Munari, for instance...

Alongside this constant feature, the temptation periodically recurs to see modernity as a quest for historical identity, to use old symbols to convey topical concerns: the Italian postmodern is wholly based on theorems that were once used by the Novecento.

The second consideration (not historical but environmental) is represented by the de-regulation of the overall system of Italian design. I am speaking of the absence of unitary and central schools of design, which has led to an input to the profession from two different sources: on the one hand from great natural talents (like Munari, for example...), and on the other from architects who received their training in faculties where design was not taught: extraordinary and skilful *naïfs*, in an environment characterised by a wide-ranging university culture.

The last consideration (though it might well be the most comprehensive of all) is that of Italian political history, where modern culture has always been in opposition, and has been associated with scandal, rupture and minority interests. Whereas in the other great democracies of Europe (Britain, Sweden, Denmark, Finland, Holland and Belgium) the Modern Movement received the accolade of official adoption, as the mark of a continuity with tradition and with social reform, in Italy it has always signified criticism, controversy and heterodoxy. As in Munari, for example...

Even the partnership between Italian design and industry has never taken place at the level of a simple functional integration, but involves rather a successful collaboration between a highly flexible manufacturing system and a design rich in unaccustomed methodologies, heedful of the languages of art and endowed with powerful figurative codes of its own.

If this has been (in broad terms) the 'mode of operation of the system of Italian design', the work of Bruno Munari cuts right across it, and in some ways represents an important key to its interpretation on an autobiographical level. Munari's work can serve not only as a formal and methodological example of the spirit of Italian design, but also a suggestive demonstration of it, of how everything can be turned into daily life and work.

In point of fact, it seems easier to describe Munari's career in terms of a design project for a mode of living, rather than in terms of a profession and an art.

Not because his life has been an extraordinary one in formal terms; indeed, it has been the opposite. His domestic and everyday character is perfectly straightforward. And it may be in this that there resides one of the most important qualities of his work: aesthetic research that produces 'normal' values in life. Almost a utopia, in which the artist and the ordinary man, for once, are not the opposite poles of an impossible duality, but coexist in harmony.

Much has been written on the subject of his continual research into signs, materials and surreal values. For Munari, reality is an all-inclusive fact, a unique system made up of bodies, but also of their shadows, double meanings and possible ambiguities. Indeed, he often discovers pleasant surprises concealed in human and technological error.

Munari often says, and rightly, that it is not research that should be purposeful, but its results. In other words, let me play, then we will see. What this comes down to is an affirmation of the scientific method, for Munari wants to have maximum freedom at the outset, wishing to understand thoroughly what kind of quality can produce the 'unthought of'. Then he wants to apply the results to design (which is again creative reflection, applied science). By doing this, he produces art applied to industry; but also industry applied to art. Pure research, but amid the compromises of daily life. Play as science, but the other way round as well. And without excluding chance.

Like the English reformers of the last century, Munari sees design as produced by a happy designer; his peace of mind

Pesci di carta pieghevoli. Allestimento vetrine La Rinascente, 1952.

Folding paper fishes. Window dressing for La Rinascente, 1952.

is indispensable to the quality of the design, and therefore of culture. Unhappiness can produce nothing but more of itself.

In 1985 he received the Award of the City of Osaka, which in Japan is equivalent to being declared a national monument. There can be no doubt that the Japanese admire in him many of their own virtues: courtesy, innocence, cunning. And there are many things in Bruno Munari that find an echo in Oriental culture, and in the Confucian virtues in particular.

In some ways Gianni Vattimo was correct in describing Munari's work as pervaded by a 'weak' mode of thought. Weak in the sense that, unlike the strong versions of design, which have marked the Western avant-garde movements of this century, committed as they were to imagining a new anthropology suited to the age of industrialism, Munari, like much of Eastern culture, has been heading in the opposite direction. That is to say, he has sought to filter technology through a gracious code, without rejecting anything but also without 'interiorising the machine', without letting himself be totally carried away by the torrid wind of industrialism. On the contrary, he has adopted the Oriental technique of ju-jitsu, which consists in assisting the force of nature or of an adversary, in order to turn it against them. To do this he does not need to be 'against' reality, but 'within' it; so as to seek out the good soul of the world, the last drops of humidity inside even the driest of stones.

And Munari, as a good Venetian-Milanese Shintoist, believes that there is a soul hidden in things, in machines or in wires; and perhaps he does not believe in death, in the existence of unusable areas of material life.

Fundamentally Munari, like those from the Orient, believes that culture does not reside in finished products, but in the act of making them. Not in the result, but in the process. Yet I do not wish to drive Munari into the arms of the East, far away from our own culture. I see in him one of the few smiling sages that we have available to us; I do not call him Master because he has always taught that it is necessary to be able to do without one. And that a child may be worth as much and perhaps even more than a great thinker, when it comes to dealing with the enigmas of the world.

Andrea Branzi

Water-mill on the Adige.

Coloured pencils on paper, 1940

5

'Suddenly, without any kind of warning, I found myself completely naked, in the heart of the city of Milan, on the morning of 24 October 1907. My father was in contact with the city's best-known personalities, being a waiter at the Gambrinus. My mother put on airs while embroidering fans.'[1]

Thus began the life of Bruno Munari, who today looks back on his parents and his birth with affectionate irony. Pia and Enrico Brunari very soon left Milan, moving with Bruno to Badia Polesine, a small town near the Adige in the Veneto region. Munari grew up there, staying until he was eighteen. When he returned to Milan to begin his artistic career, Munari had no regular studies behind him, but he did have an enormous reserve of natural influences, influences which were to mould the whole of his subsequent output.
His parents converted a small mansion, formerly the country residence of the Dukes of Este, into a hotel. Munari has recently confessed — during an interview with Andrea Branzi — that he does not look back on that work with pleasure: 'I lived a hotel life, giving a hand to my father, but I did not enjoy it because it was a life without rest. If you weren't relieved you had to go to bed at two o'clock in the morning, when the last guest had come in, and get up at five to go and lay in supplies. My mother came up with a definition for this, saying that you had to sleep in a hurry.'

Luckily, country life had very different emotions in store for the young Munari, who used to play with other children — naturally unaware that he would still be doing so seventy years later — and discovered both nature and the pleasure of imitating and modifying it: 'Since childhood I have been an experimenter, even when I was making toys for myself or my friends, using bamboo canes or other lowly materials. I have always been curious to see what else could be done with something, apart from its normal use.'[2]

Munari at Badia Polesine.

The poultry-man on his way back from market.

Thanks to an uncle who was a lute-maker (and cook), the young Munari was exposed to sinuous and harmonious forms.

At Badia Polesine people grew beet and raised silkworms. Cartoon, pencil on paper, 1932.

Underlying Munari's creative imagination is an enchanted childhood, spent along the Great River and among its machines, among the organic forms of nature and the forms produced by peasant craftsmen from simple materials. The water-mill, scarecrows made out of reeds from the river, the movements of water, and the local market combined to form the imaginative heritage of the artist.

Golf on the bank of the Adige: Munari is about to make a putt.

The low-lying landscape of the Veneto region, criss-crossed by rows of trees, held a great wealth of experience in reserve for Bruno: 'From the top of the bank the sight took our breath away, partly because we had climbed up there in a hurry. And our Machine was there, floating on the water near the river bank: an old wooden mill that looked as if it had been built by Robinson Crusoe.
'The sky was immense and the wind ruffled our hair; the great mass of grey water of the Adige flowed slowly past, tracing out dangerous whirlpools here and there. For me and my friends that water came from the unknown and went towards the unknown, bearing pieces of wood and dead branches, tufts of grass and uprooted bushes, sometimes strange objects and dead cats.
'One by one we crossed the narrow wooden gangplank linking the mill to the bank, and we were on the raft. This was made out of a large number of planks fastened together and supported by two large pontoons. In the middle of the raft stood the shed with its straw roof. Next to the shed, on the river side, the Great Wheel slowly turned. The whole Machine was made out of old wood turned grey, with its grain made to stand out by the effects of wind and weather; only the metal pivots of the wheel and the grindstones shone brightly, polished by the continual friction, in the semi-darkness of the shed, surrounded by floury cobwebs and full sacks with human shapes. All the Machine creaked, groaned, sighed, rumbled and gurgled and you could make out the rhythms largely produced by the rotation of the wheel.
The Great Wheel was an ever-changing spectacle: with measured slowness it fished up wonderful weeds and water plants green as soft glass, making them shine in the sun, raising them as high as it could and then lowering them still slowly, immersing them again in a glittering spray with the sound of scattered and continuous rain acting as a background to the other noises of the mill. Every so often you noticed the smell of flour and weed, of water and earth, of dry wood and musk. And once in a while the Great Wheel brought up a chicken feather or piece of paper or the leaf of a tree along with the water plants to vary its patterns of greenery.
'And while my friends swarmed over every accessible corner of the mill, trying to break down the door of the shed and throwing stones at water birds, I was there, near the Great Wheel, with the river water passing continually beneath the planks on which I stood, as if suspended in the air, admiring the uninterrupted spectacle of colours, light and the movements of the Great Wheel.'[3]

Negative positive, oil on board, 1950
The Great Machine on the river.

Negativo positivo, olio su tavola, 1950.

La Grande Macchina sul fiume.

TULLIO D'ALBISOLA · ORIANI · THAYAHT · BOT · SPANO · DIULGHEROFF · LINO PESARO · PRAMPOLINI · ESCODAMÈ · MUNARI · FILLIA

MARINETTI

Futurists at the Galleria Pesaro, 1932.

On his arrival in Milan, Munari at once came into contact with Futurists from the second wave of the movement. With them, Munari, who was most influenced by Balla and Prampolini, carried out research into all the possibilities of creative action, action that could be translated into practical results in any field of visual operation. Apart from Futurism, he immediately tried his hand, without any preconceptions, at Cubism, metaphysical art and Surrealism. In his early period he showed a preference for compositions made up of 'conical' forms, which can be seen not only in his drawings and paintings, but also in his ceramic works of the period.

This evocative passage also contains a list of what would turn out to be Munari's greatest interests as an adult. The Heraclitan notion 'everything flows' passed before his childish eyes and left as a permanent mark the influence of nature in movement, the action of wind and water — beautiful in themselves, but important too because they introduce variety into the beauty of the landscape. And then, the interference of man, or rather of the manmade machine, a machine built to work and not to provide entertainment, whose regular rhythms derive from a mechanism bent by man to productive ends. And yet those rhythms, in their interaction with nature, with chance, took on a contemplative value.

Some of Munari's remarks already denote a bias towards rational, technical observation, others a leaning towards the surreal ('water plants green as soft glass'). The passage is an important one since from here on we will often come across the themes listed in it. Still involved in his memories, Munari rediscovers his own discontent as a restless adolescent, racked by the burning desire to do something that would reach beyond the bounds of rural horizons: 'Before the war travelling salesmen would pass by

and stop for one or two nights, and it was one of them who told me about Futurism. I remember that he had a kerchief around his neck, something strange because in those days people only wore shirts with a tie, and I was enthralled; I was about eighteen, and had started to make drawings, but without knowing anything, just inventing. I had two friends who were painters, Gino Visentini and Gelindo Furlan. They went around with their paint-boxes, and I went with them, to paint landscapes. But, while this was going on, I was also playing lots of games with the water and I don't know what.'[4]

So Munari was born in Milan and Milan was to be the centre of all his artistic activity. But one cannot overlook — establishing his roots and the influences on his art — the years spent in the Veneto, alongside the river which never ceased flowing and at every moment brought new information, for those who knew how to see it; in the market-place, with the great sheets onto which silkworms were turned out for sale; among the scarecrows invented and constructed by farmers; by the mill, a great machine that was at once useful and useless. And within him that wholly provincial desire to discover the world and act in it.

The wall reserved for Munari at the Futurist collective exhibition held at the Galleria Pesaro in 1929.

1926: Bruno Munari arrived in Milan, a great industrial city even if it was not yet a metropolis — a city for which Munari feels a profound love since it has always permitted him to accomplish what he desired.

There was an uncle waiting for him in Milan. He was an engineer, and he helped the young Munari by giving him work in his studio. Here he began to earn a living, from then on always remaining faithful to the principle of doing a job (adman, art director, illustrator) from which he could earn a living, so that he was not always tied to the art market and dependent on it financially. Thus he was able to hang on to his own independence. It was an important choice, for it freed him from the temptation to create a style of his own, easily recognisable in the art market but in the long run sterile. At the same time it allowed him to escape tiresome frustrations over possible (and actual) lack of understanding. Hence the figure cut by the twenty-year-old Munari was already that of an artist who wanted nothing at all to do with romanticism.

He carried on with his halting artistic experiments in Milan. From this period date a number of drawings, little more than sketches, that reflect the influence of Surrealism. Munari's first encounter with the Futurists of Milan makes an amusing story. As Munari tells it: 'The first person whom I met, going around the bookshops, was a Futurist poet who called himself Escodamé. His real name was Lescovich, but since under Fascism foreign names were frowned on, he changed it to Escodamé. He had an antiquarian bookshop — a strange contrast for a Futurist — and I had gone there to ask about a certain book that was on display in the window, for it had drawings that intrigued me. He talked to me for a while, then asked me if I knew the Futurists. I said no, but that I would like to get to know them. Then he told me he would introduce me to Marinetti who would come to stay in Milan at the Trianon, the hotel Marinetti frequented whenever he came to Milan, after sending warning of his arrival by telegram.'

Munari mentions Balla and Prampolini as among the Futurists who had the greatest influence on him. And in fact they are two key names in the Futurist movement (which years of research and study have at last rehabilitated), both in its early version (during the second decade of the century) and in its later phase, during the 1920s and 1930s.

Early Futurism, as represented by Marinetti, Boccioni, Carrà and Sant'Elia, but also by Balla, Depero and Prampolini, marked a fundamental break not only in the history of the avant-garde, but in that of contemporary art. Although Munari worked in the ambit of the second wave of Futurism (it should be remembered that the label of Futurism, whether that of the first or second phase, covers groups or tendencies that often differed greatly from each other), it is in early Futurism, and especially that of Balla, that one must look for his artistic origins. For Munari, with his innate capacity for experimentation, the pictorial or plastic research of Boccioni or Carrà could not be sufficient, however fundamental it may have been; on the other hand he felt completely at home with the motivations of those — like Balla, Depero and Prampolini — who had put forward the idea of a 'Futurist reconstruction of the universe'. It is this idea, this plan, that appears irrefutably today to be 'the indispensable key to interpretation of the Futurist experience as a whole as well as to the implications of its individual movements' (Crispolti).[6] Even a quick glance at the manifesto *Ricostruzione futurista dell'universo*, published by Balla and Depero in Milan in 1915, reveals Munari in a nutshell. The use of lowly materials: 'Metal wires, cotton threads ... coloured glass, onionskin paper ... transparent wire meshes of all kinds ... mechanical and electrical devices, etc.' The longing to achieve movement: 'Three-dimensional groups that turn on a pivot ... on several pivots, etc.'

The interest in toys, which should no longer 'bewilder and dishearten the child' but get him used to 'laughing quite openly ... to the greatest elasticity ... to the leap of

11

Constructing, tempera on board, 1929.

Self-portrait, tempera on paper, 1930.

imagination ... to reaching out infinitely and to making supple his sensitivity'.

When Balla and Depero described the properties of their dynamic three-dimensional assembly, they listed eleven points of which at least seven are perfectly suited to Munari's later works: abstract, dynamic, highly transparent, brightly coloured and luminous, autonomous (i.e. resembling nothing but itself), changeable and volatile. And Balla seemed to hint at the repeatability, the multiplication of his works when he wrote: 'the physical construction of the three-dimensional assembly. Necessary means...'.[7] This trend in Futurism provides other themes in Munari's work — such as those supplied by the contemplation of nature — which indicate that he has never been out of touch with developments in contemporary art, even though he has handled them in his own completely original manner.

At this point we would like to add another appellation to the many, often vague and imprecise, that Munari has collected over his career: more than a creator, Munari is a 'reconstructor', for he always sets out from reality, drawing attention to its unfamiliar aspects.

When Munari joined the Futurist movement, after his encounter with Marinetti, it was its more practical trend that had the greatest influence on him. In that period Italian art, like that of Europe in general, had just seen the collapse of the avant-garde movements, the breakdown of Dada into Surrealism, of Surrealism into itself; the difficulties encountered by Russian and German artists for political reasons; the call for a 'return to order' that was being raised by authoritative artists. On the Italian peninsula it had seen the birth of a variety of conservative schools and tendencies and, finally, the crisis in Futurism itself. But times were changing, and the heroic period of Futurism was over. Given up for dead, along with Boccioni and Sant'Elia — killed during the Great War — Futurism managed to survive, first by indulging in mechanical fantasies and then, during the course of the 1930s, by effectively turning its attention to the present and the new problems it raised, applying imagination to the handling of concrete matters. Today's concerns were the new preoccupation, and no longer a reaching out towards the future. It was against this active background, although pervaded by metaphysical, surrealistic and abstract tendencies, that Munari's ideas were moulded. From 1927 to 1936 he took an active part in Futurist exhibitions in Milan, at the Venice Biennale or the Quadriennale in Rome, and in Paris. Munari's Futurism presents an irregular appearance, difficult to single out for examination. This is partly due to the loss of many of his works dating from this period, because they had been executed on humble and perishable materials. However, a number of drawings and a few photographs — some of which are published here for the first time — have survived, allowing

Tempera on paper, 1932.

us to document his artistic development as completely as possible. It should be said that this development was largely in line with the trends of the day, but it also demonstrates the flexibility with which Munari has maintained his relations with artistic movements, and which has ensured the incredible longevity of his artistic career and the constant freshness of his creative approach. The twenty-year-old Munari had to sever his connections with painting and immediately embarked on the latest pictorial variation of Futurism, painting with an airbrush. A few paintings from this period, such as *Building* (1928), reveal the odd rehashed link with Cubism. But there are also signs — as far as it is possible to tell from a few faded photographs — of a propensity towards Surrealism, but a Surrealism checked by metaphysical estrangement, or by a cool constructivist approach.

But what needs stressing now is Munari's devotion to nature, especially against an artistic background that tended towards the mechanical or towards a break out into cosmic space. In his paintings we often find open, peaceful skies, inhabited by strange presences or dense traceries of brushwork (a visual feature that continued to crop up even into the 1950s), as in the work made with different materials *Adventure on pink sky*. At times Munari put on a Futurist camouflage, but his painting almost always seems to be striving to go beyond. On the other hand the theme or pretext of his drawings — which have survived in greater numbers — is the human figure, at rest, in movement, often grotesque and still more often fused with elements of the plant world. Structures of lines surface and these appear to hold the morphological elements of his sketches together. Even in his surrealistic works there is a strong interest in natural structures, or rather, in the structure of the things that are accurately reproduced on the paper (this is probably also the reason why a great deal of space is given in his photomontages to the structured components of the human body: the nervous system, the circulation of the blood, the skeleton). Almost throughout the 1930s Munari's paintings and illustrations bore the mark of Prampolini's influence — when he did not free himself of it by painting abstract pictures or seeking new directions.

Enrico Prampolini, who had his own idea of the Futurist reconstruction of the universe as far back as 1915, was one of the main links between the first and second phases of Futurism. If what Crispolti has written is true, that 'Prampolini's "cosmic idealism" is anything but a revival of Boccioni, having... the aim of establishing a dialogue with "parasurrealist" positions in new European art, the influence of which can be detected in Fillia, Oriani, Benedetta herself, or in Tano, for example',[8] it is also true that these influence extended as far as Munari.

But there can be no question that Munari was an exponent of the second wave of Futurism in Milan, and by no means a minor one. As early as 1927, in a curious collaboration with Aligi Sassu, only fifteen at the time, Munari drew up the manifesto *Dinamismo e forza muscolare* (Dynamism and muscular strength). This took a distinctly anti-academic stand (in opposition above all to the Novecento, the artistic movement whose reactionary attitudes dominated the Italian artistic scene in those years): the two young painters were demanding a new mechanical, animal and vegetable world.

In fact what has survived from the period also testifies to the influence of 'mechanisation' in the style of Pannaggi or Paladini — as in Marinetti's drawings for *The naked prompter*, or other scattered drawings. But his painting and his works employing different materials, as we have seen, were more rooted in the metaphysical and surrealistic field than in the rigidly mechanical one, while his plastic art — such as the 1930 *Aerial machine* — was a decided foreshadowing of 'concretist' research. So it must be said that, apart from his 'external' Futurism, devoid of any major results, Munari was 'internally' a Futurist. In fact he was to become more of a Futurist when Futurism was already dead than when he was working as an official member of the movement. And yet his was the driving force in the Futurist group based in Milan, where he took part in numerous joint exhibitions and where — along with Andreoni, Duse, Manzoni, Gambini and Bot — he drew up its manifesto in 1932. Among other things, this had the following to say: 'Abolishing all perspective and primitive

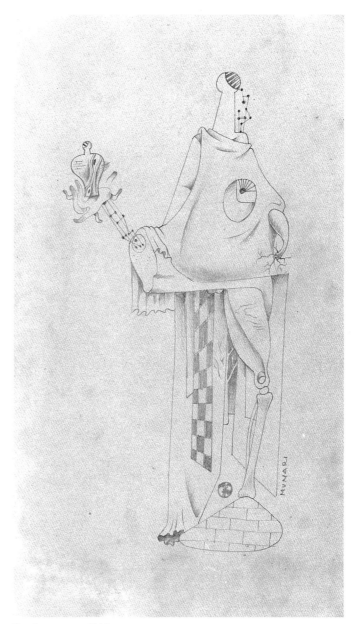

Pencil on paper, 1934.

During his period of Futurist militancy — which was not free from dispute, even with Marinetti, with whom he often collaborated — Munari managed to skip any form of academic training, immediately setting himself to work in the fields of advertising, graphics, illustration, interior decoration, photography and the cinema. Munari soon learned to work by eliminating intellectual superstructures, thanks in part to his application of specific techniques, whose creative possibilities he exploited to the maximum, without regard for style.

plastics in order to build the new picture with elements of perspective and chromatic plastics. Hence knowing how to distinguish the colours that are alive for us in our own age ... from colours belonging to other ages ... which produce pictorial infection and thence the more or less rapid demise of artistic systems'.[9]

Like the more gifted painters and theoreticians of the art of painting with an airbrush — Prampolini and Fillia — Munari abandoned the illustrative view of painting, searching for new paths that would lead him towards new pictorial structures.

Self-portrait, Indian ink on paper, 1930.

Painter at the easel, Indian ink on paper, 1937.

15

Tempera on paper, 1932.

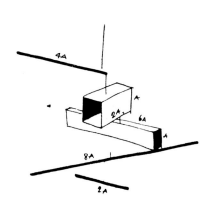

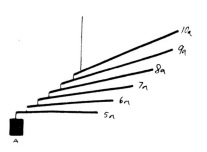

Designs for *Useless machines*, pencil on paper, 1940.

Throughout the 1930s Munari was influenced by Surrealism, although he managed to bring these influences to bear in the direction of design or of outright Dada. Fascinated by a view of the human body as a machine, one of his sources of inspiration was an anatomical atlas made up of superimposable transparent sheets, a device that he was later to adopt in the make-up of his own books.
In the spirit of the time were his mixtures of vegetable and animal sources, which led him to research the basic structures of natural organisms. His Surrealist compositions, however, were very often the outcome of a combination of different techniques.

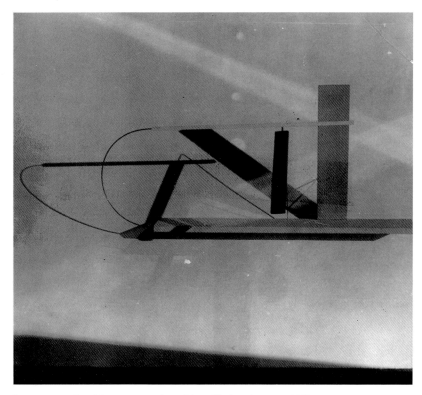

Sensitive, wood and iron construction with oscillating elements, 1937.

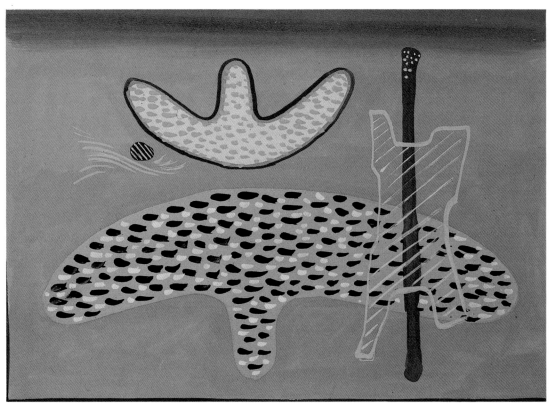

Tempera on paper, 1932.

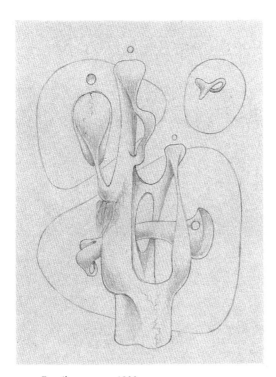

Pencil on paper, 1930.

Collage, 1940.

Collage, 1940.

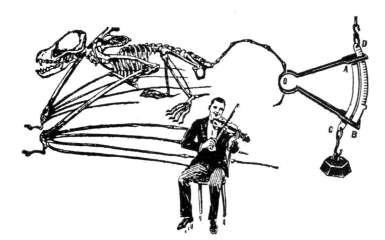

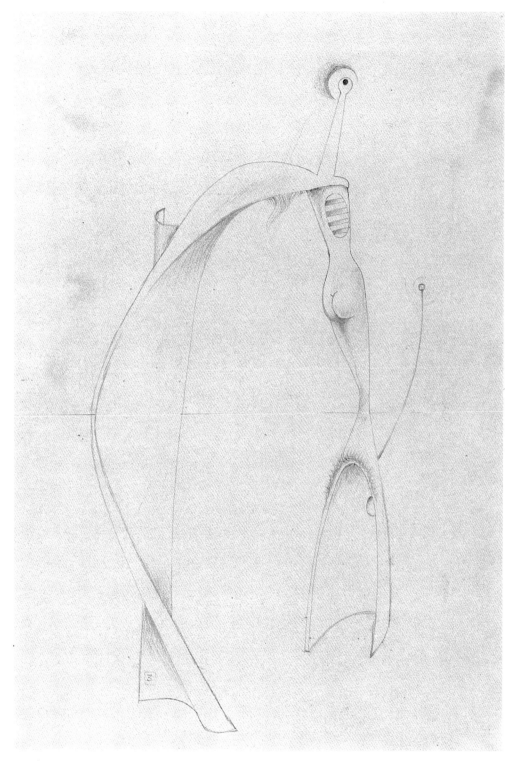

Pencil on paper, 1936.

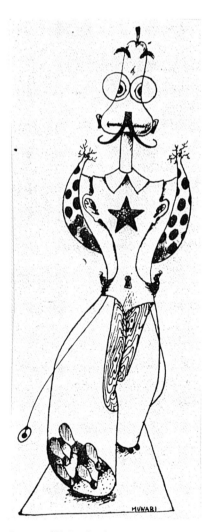

Portrait of Tullio d'Albisola,
pencil on paper, 1935.

19

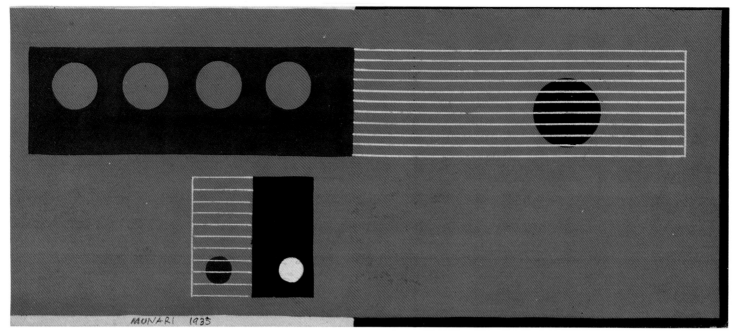

The frame too, tempera on board, 1935.

Again, in the *Manifesto tecnico dell'aeroplastica futurista*
(Technical manifesto of futurist aeroplastics) of 1930 (with
Manzoni, Furlan, Ricas and Regina), Munari theorises
about alternative modes of expression to painting and
sculpture, proposing, in a remarkable anticipation of 'land
art', working directly on the land, 'diverting rivers
constructing woods lakes meadows air water earth in
accordance with new landscape designs that will glorify
over the centuries ... the immense joy of being alive.'[10]
From Futurism to abstraction was but a short step, and
Munari did not draw back from it. Already in his *Aerial
machine* of 1930, made up of rods, spheres and semicircles
painted in red and white, there was a hint of his celebrated
Useless machines.
But what links did Munari have with the most interesting
experiments involving abstraction at that time? Once again
the name of Prampolini crops up; Prampolini the
indefatigable traveller who served as a point of contact
between the Futurists and Mondrian. But he was not the
only one, given that news about what was going on in the
rest of Europe arrived through the circulation of prestigious
foreign reviews, such as *Abstraction-Création* and *Cercle et
Carré*, where Munari could find reproductions of works and
theoretical writings by Mondrian, Arp, Kandinsky and
many other protagonists of European art. Nor must one
forget the fundamental influence of the *Bauhausbücher*,
which recorded the experiences of the school of Gropius.

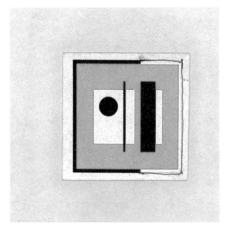

The frame too, tempera on board, 1935.

His experience with Futurism, which involved a
considerable degree of freedom, rapidly pushed Munari
in the direction of abstraction, but an abstraction that
was free of formalist dogmas. Evidence of this is to be
found in a series of three tempera paintings entitled
The frame too, where the painting invades the structure
that traditionally excludes it from ordinary space.
Having given much thought to the lessons imparted by
Mondrian, Munari, an attentive reader of publications
on art from all over Europe, found in Josef Albers and
Laszlo Moholy-Nagy, young teachers at the Bauhaus,
the closest parallels to his own experimentation, along
with an important link to Russian constructivism.

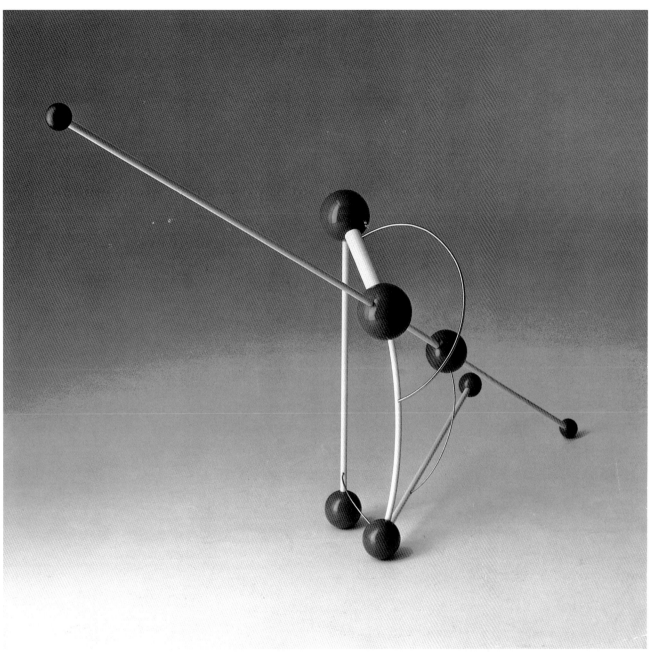

Aerial machine, red spheres and white shafts in wood, curves in steel, 1930 (reconstruction for Danese, 1971).

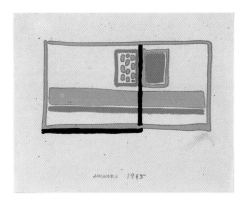

Tempera on paper, 1945.

On top of all this came the opening of the Galleria del Milione in 1932, centre of the so-called 'Lombard abstractionism'. Although he never belonged to the group officially, it was often visited by Munari. The young painter was greatly struck by Mondrian, in whose pictures he discovered the total structural value of elements. In Mondrian he recognised the first artist to come up with colour and form that were solely an expression of themselves. And he was intrigued by Mondrian's precision, for Munari was already involved in a search for the objective, in an attempt to eliminate 'states of mind' from the finished product.

In his figurative drawings and sketches he had already shown a clear interest in structure, in the skeleton of that sort of cross between human being and plant that often

bordered on the caricature, on the surreal. And this was
not all: there are many montages, both photographic and
graphic, from the 1930s in which Munari inserted
structures, organs of the human body, seeming to
investigate them both as machines and in order to break
them down for purely Surrealist purposes. So Munari was
already aiming at the essential, at a form pared down to its
most basic terms, and this explains his interest in the
battle fought by Mondrian against Expressionism and the
'modern baroque': on the one hand by the attempt to
denaturalise painting so as to reduce it to its raw elements,
for only in this way can painting have a specific nature of
its own; on the other by the attempt to bring life into art,
so that 'life itself pushes art over the precipice', for only
then 'will art be transformed, be realised first in our
tangible surroundings, then in society' (Mondrian).[11]
The latter aspect, in fact, one detects in Munari's work
mainly after the war, when he began to concentrate on
industrial design. But it is certain that Mondrian freed
himself from the decorative and useless, which for Munari
meant from excess of expression, i.e. a phenomenon of
redundancy, the absence of background noise which was
superfluous to communication. That Munari was also
concerned with the essence of artistic work, with its
autonomy, is proved by his experiments with the
photogram, the photograph made without a camera,
involving a procedure that takes the photographic medium
back to 'writing with light', which transforms it into a
verification of its means and language.
Munari too aimed to bring art into life, on the outside,
and therefore he worked a discourse into his art, into its
technical means and linguistic structures. That Munari was
also an uneasy abstractionist is demonstrated by his
impatience with the artistic means. Out of this impatience,
and his search for the essential structures of the picture,
emerged a series of brilliant solutions, above all that of the
Useless machines.

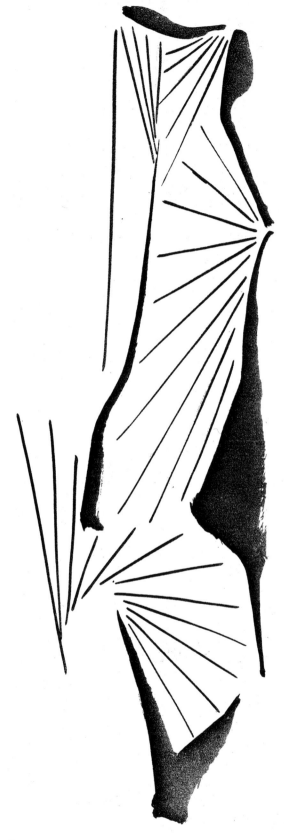

Tempera on paper, 1940.

Coloured pencils on tracing paper, 1929.

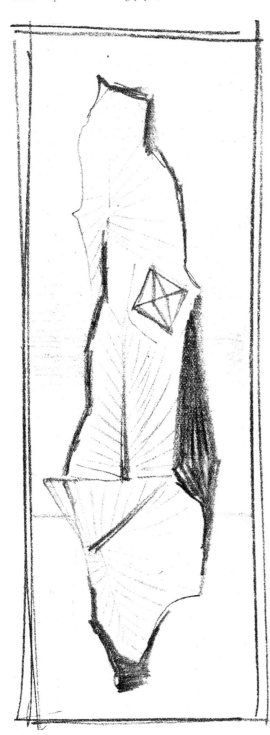

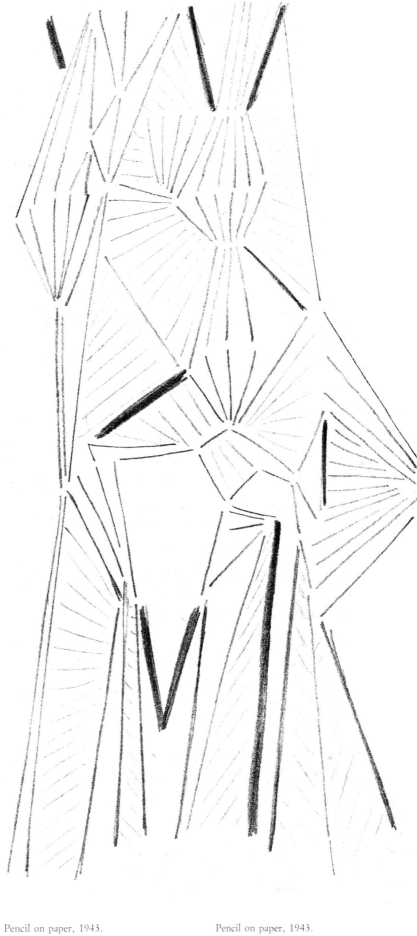

23

Pencil on paper, 1943.   Pencil on paper, 1943.

Cartoon, pencil on paper, 1930.

For a Futurist to tackle the theme of the machine was normal. Throughout Munari's life, it was almost a matter of daily bread for him, as we shall see. In a comic drawing made in 1930 we find, though naturally just as a joke, the theme of the machine used for artistic purposes: a robot which is painting a rather flowery sort of birth of Venus. It is a minor drawing, but it deals with a central feature of Munari's art. At the same time it belongs to a minor branch of his output — the easel painting — in which he continued to dabble up until 1940. In any case it is the painter looking into his own work.

The machine, then, can be considered as work of art or artist: but Munari's machines are no longer Futurist, with that touch of Expressionism and drama that is typical of the mechanisation of the 1920s. Munari decided they should be pacific machines instead, not representing a possible future, but merely themselves, through their colours and the movement of forms, and thus through their entry into reality, into life. This was how Munari's *Useless machines* were born, his most popular work up to the present day. To enable us to understand how the theme of the machine shifted from Futurism to abstractionism, let the artist explain in his own words: 'The first abstract pictures were painted in Italy in 1933. They were nothing but geometric forms and coloured spaces without any reference to external nature ... Personally I thought that, instead of painting squares, triangles or other geometric shapes within the still verist atmosphere (one thinks of Kandinsky) of a picture, it would have been interesting to free the abstract forms from the immobility of the painting and suspend them in the air, linked together so that they would share our surroundings with us, sensitive to the true atmosphere of reality...

'I don't know if Calder started out from the same principle, but the fact is that we both found ourselves endorsing a move from figurative art in two or three dimensions to the fourth dimension: time.'[12]

His first *Useless machines*, which qualify as machines in that they are levers, although only of the first degree, date back to 1933. Thus Munari achieved a completely structural nature for all the elements of the work, the introduction of art into life, a true kinetics. As well as his roots in Futurism and nature, the influence of a number of European masters was decisive in persuading him to move from Futurism to abstraction; this indicated that he was

Tempera on canvas, 1932.

Left: *Useless machine*, wood and silk thread, 1934.

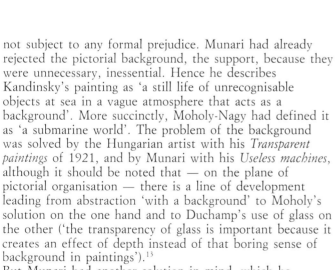

Tempera and collage on canvas, 1932.

not subject to any formal prejudice. Munari had already rejected the pictorial background, the support, because they were unnecessary, inessential. Hence he describes Kandinsky's painting as 'a still life of unrecognisable objects at sea in a vague atmosphere that acts as a background'. More succinctly, Moholy-Nagy had defined it as 'a submarine world'. The problem of the background was solved by the Hungarian artist with his *Transparent paintings* of 1921, and by Munari with his *Useless machines*, although it should be noted that — on the plane of pictorial organisation — there is a line of development leading from abstraction 'with a background' to Moholy's solution on the one hand and to Duchamp's use of glass on the other ('the transparency of glass is important because it creates an effect of depth instead of that boring sense of background in paintings').[13]

But Munari had another solution in mind, which he reached with the series of three paintings entitled *The frame too* and in which his reaction to Moholy-Nagy and Josef Albers is most clearly felt. These paintings, in white, black and red, reveal a familiarity with the best European practices of the time and fully justify Munari's claim to be one of the protagonists of Italian abstractionism. But that he is critical in his attitude towards the latter is

demonstrated by his inclusion of the frame in the field of the painting; a deliberate inclusion, borne out by the title (Munari's titles are always important and never just labels). Evidently, purely abstract research did not satisfy Munari, who was by then convinced that art should live in the world of men, in phenomenological reality and the flux of things. By also painting the element that separates — both physically and symbolically — the painting from the world, Munari made the former fit into the latter. His visual research was directed towards the creation of an integral three-dimensional space, where everything comes together in a perceptual ambiguity for an effect of depth and relief. As has been pointed out, this results in 'an animation of amplitudes and tensions that are no longer opposed to each other but contiguous and continuous, echoing, implicating and altering each other in ceaseless turn, like the whole in its phenomenological fragrance, grasped at different points'.[14]

A few years later, in 1937, came the painting *A blue point*, a 'free cascade of forms and colours' (Caramel). Do not be misled by the total diversity of expression in these brushstrokes with regard to the geometrical and perceptual rigour of his previous paintings. *A blue point* proves that Munari was still interested in saying something about art

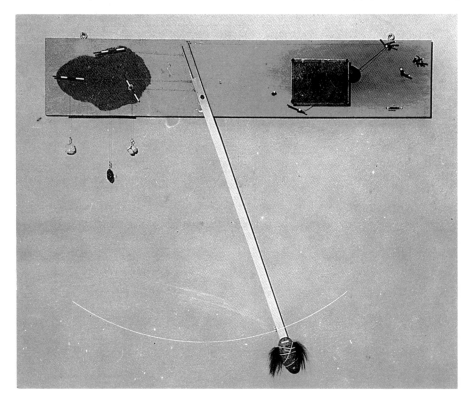

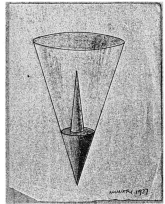

Portrait of Russolo, coloured pencils, 1927.

Machine's breath, various materials, 1938.

by investigating its means, in this case simple brush-strokes, of different colours and sizes but identical force — reminiscent perhaps of the Pointillists or Balla — that are merely placed on the surface; the primary forms of painting that in the end create the perception of a three-dimensional space in two dimensions.

It will be noticed that Munari was working with different means of expression over the same period. Moreover, having once rejected the support, ground and frame, he was still able to return to 'traditional' painting. Having once pursued a particular line of research, Munari rarely made any attempt to exhaust it completely. This gives rise to a problem for the critics: how to put Munari into perspective? In reality, this is simply not possible, for no particular line of research was predominant. There were simply periods in which he was more interested and carried out more research in one field than another. Munari has almost never devoted himself completely to a single line of research, so that it would be possible to look on him as a Futurist, a Surrealist, a metaphysician, an abstractionist or a kineticist. Even a designer or a writer. But it would always be a partial view of him. Indeed, it is his *Useless machines* that give a more complex and accurate idea of

Munari's world, the world that we have begun to sketch out. In fact the *Useless machines* function as his world, forming a system in which the elimination of one element would cause a break-down in the highly delicate equilibrium; an equilibrium obtained by balancing the elements in harmonious relationships with one another. They spurn fixity and the frame; they may require the intervention of the spectator, allowing him to carry out a check; they represent nothing but themselves and the space they create through their tranquil movement; they produce nothing, except aesthetic pleasure; they can be mass-produced (Munari explains how): functionally they can be reduced to two-dimensionality and to the minimum basic space obtained with a module, in spite of their having rejected the two dimensions of the picture (and this is an irony).

In Munari, *tout se tient*. And, returning to our chronological digression, it can be said that, on the threshold of the 1940s, Munari did not plunge himself single-mindedly into a particular line of research, but began to explore numerous channels, although without ever losing himself.

Airbrush paintings and *Useless machines* in
Munari's studio, early 1930s.

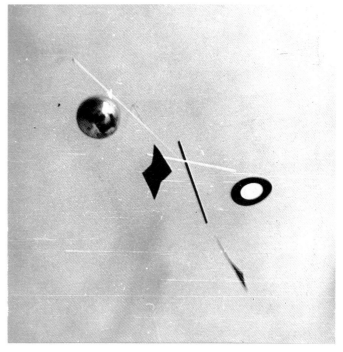

One of the first *Useless machines* in movement.

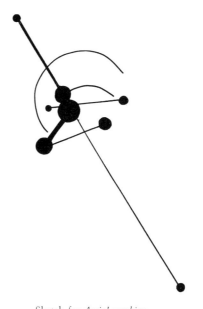

Sketch for *Aerial machine*,
pencil on paper, 1930.

The legacy of his childhood, his Futurist experiments
with a variety of materials, his direct experience of
production techniques and his appreciation of the modern
and of machinery gave Munari a particular taste for
trying out various materials. His paintings on new
materials (masonite), the creation of objects (like *Sensitive*)
endowed with a 'natural' sensitivity and of the *Useless
machines* made out of very ordinary materials, all acted as
a prelude to his work, after the war, on materials in the
sphere of industrial design.

Cover for *Il poema del vestito di latte*, by Marinetti, 1937.

Bruno Munari in the 1930s was not simply an innovator concerned with painting and other visual activities, such as photography, photomontage, photograms and film. Having grown up under the influence of the second wave of Futurism, he decided to invade art with life, and vice versa.

Since 1929, Munari had also been working in the field of advertising, as graphic designer in a variety of studios. These included Cossio's IPC, pioneer in the use of the animated cartoon in Italian advertising. In collaboration with Cossio, Munari produced a number of animated advertisements, making use of cartoon figures cut out of cardboard, fixed with pins and photographed frame by frame. The following year Munari opened, together with Riccardo Ricas, who for some time shared his artistic ideas, an advertising studio. This was one of the first advertising studios in Italy, but rather different from the modern agencies, seeing that its two directors also handled the decoration of interiors and buildings. At the same time as he was exhibiting with the Futurists and making an approach to abstract painting, Munari, in his work as a graphic artist, had to deal with page make-up, type and covers: out of this came his long experience in this field. Apart from the early influence of Prampolini — as can be seen in the cover he designed for Masnata's *Anime sceneggiate* — it was the work of Herbert Bayer, director of the graphic section of the Bauhaus and familiar to Munari chiefly through the *Bauhausbücher*, that played the greatest part in moulding his talent. We have an example of this in the make-up of *L'Ufficio moderno* (1935). Lettering, spacing and columns were far from traditional, in comparison with magazines of the day. A swarm of blue brush-strokes even invades the page, without any explanatory caption, disturbing the equilibrium between a photograph and the space surrounding it. Behind this lay twenty years of Futurist graphics, but set against the background of the logical syntax of functionalism.

In that period, Munari worked for the leaders in the field of Italian graphics: the review *Campo grafico*, and the Studio Boggeri, for whom he also designed a trade-mark. He drew on all the new artistic tendencies and their accompanying techniques, without exception. In his advertising plates one finds metaphysical bewilderment or Futurist simultaneity, but the subjects are always made up accurately and cleanly, so that they can produce the desired result: clear and effective communication, that also takes the psychological aspects of the message into account. Hence Munari did not 'paint', but made up into pages, unlike many other artists involved in advertising at that time, did not became infatuated with a style but used the structural possibilities of typography, looking for an unusual use of cliché, composing directly with the screen, or employing a typeface that was new at the time, such as Renner's *Futura*. We still have examples of his work for the Campari firm: advertisements ('L'ora del Campari') and posters, like the famous one of 1965 made up of variations of the Campari logo. Along with Munari's modern and

imaginative precision often comes a reference to the human figure: the resemblance between Italy and a boot; the schematised reproduction of the process of vision in the trade-mark for the Studio Boggeri; the A and the M of the Marelli trade-mark, which become the lower and upper parts of the human body.

His work with a variety of magazines, both as a graphic designer and as an illustrator, also began in 1929. We have mentioned the influence of Bayer, but Moholy-Nagy should not be forgotten either; the latter may have acted as an intermediary between Munari and Russian constructivism. Indeed, another important influence was the Russian El Lissitsky, who wrote 'words on the printed page are to be looked at, not heard ... The arrangement of space in the book by constituent material in accordance with the laws of typographic mechanics should correspond to the content's tensions of traction and pressure'.[1] It was El Lissitsky who designed and made up *The Two Squares*, 'a book for children where the squares live through a story that progressively constructs its own symbols and its own visual metaphors and that is told through these alone, without captions' (Quintavalle).[2] These were the influences that led him to compose a *Range of typographical possibilities* (1935). One of his best works from the period was his design treatment for the *Poem of the dress of milk* by Marinetti (1937), then recently returned from his

Photomontage, 1938.

exploits in the disastrous Ethiopian venture. Munari allowed his illustrations to invade page and text, but above all he dared, for the first time, to insert a transparent sheet that, superimposed on the following page, doubled its forms and content. It is a device that 'breaks through' the opacity of the page and makes it light and loose, like a line of verse set free among ninety-nine triplets. In a similar vein, he had liberated the forms of painting into the atmosphere with his *Useless machines* and, by painting *The frame too*, had absolved it of responsibility for enclosing the picture.

Design for the cover of *Le macchine di Munari*, 1941.

He returned to this approach many times in the following years, in books for children or the *Libri illeggibili* (Unreadable books), where what counted was the story told through the possibilities of typography, and not of literature. In 1940 Munari organised a section on graphics at the 7th Triennial Exhibition in Milan, presenting the most significant of Italian and European experiences. These could not be fitted into this or that tendency, but derived instead from a new conception of graphics, one that sought an autonomous language of its own that would allow it to break away from its close ties with various artistic movements.

Like many artists caught up in avant-garde developments, Munari got involved with the theatre as well. In 1936 Munari exhibited some 'toy theatres' at the Triennal Exhibition in Milan. In these the set was designed to frame the stage with a lower and an upper panel, so that only the middle part of it was visible — an idea that recalls that of Marinetti for *Le basi* (1915) and which was taken up by Munari only as a project. In 1935, however, he had already done the set-design for a ballet that was reminiscent of Oskar Schlemmer's productions: the dancers were supposed to use stilts in order to establish, with their mechanical movements, an internal rapport between man and space. But the movements envisaged seemed to represent a sort of typographical ballet, like a page (the back-drop) on which black lines (the stilts) formed different combinations. Another project, again from 1935, harks back to Marinetti's *Manifesto del teatro totale delle masse* (Manifesto of total theatre for the masses) (1933), illustrated for the Bompiani Yearbook by Munari himself. In it, the Futurist leader challenged 'the fixed or revolving stage of contemporary theatres' that evokes a 'cage for birds, imprisoned by the back-drop and with the illusion of freedom in the proscenium arch'.[3] Perhaps Munari recalled this statement and provocatively chose to close off the proscenium with long bars. The actors-cum-acrobats were to wear costumes (dark pink behind, emerald green in front) and their task was to leap from one swing to another, like gigantic birds in a cage. Acrobatics, then, on the one hand, and the effect of a coloured pattern in the 'surface' of the stage on the other. It should be noted that one feature of these productions — which were never staged — was the idea of reducing to the minimum the structures of the set, all of which were designed to be easy to dismantle and reassemble and above all could be folded to take up little space. Munari was already aware that all forms of art and entertainment could be carried out in practice — and that all such works are also concrete objects, that take up actual space, and not just representations of ideas. Hence he was interested in everything that could be shifted, moved or transported, and wanted this to be done in the most practical and simple manner.

To gain a complete view of Munari's activity in the field of set-design we have to move on to 1963, when he produced the scenery for four one-act plays of the Nō theatre. 'The set,' one reads in the introduction, 'takes into

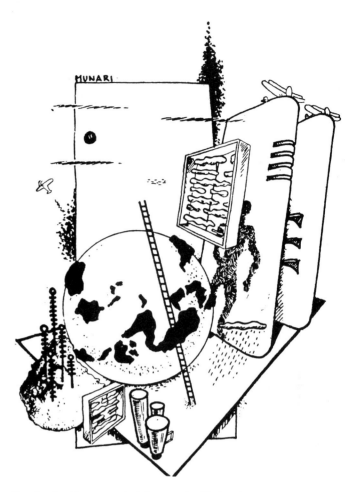

Drawing for *Il teatro totale delle masse*, by Marinetti, 1933.

Although confined to a small number of designs and realisations, Munari's activity in the realm of set-designs was in keeping with his fundamental interests: the search for specific languages, 'anti-literariness', the link with historical avant-garde movements and attention to essentials.

consideration the typical "space" of Japanese visual art, i.e. of that void that takes its appearance from the intensity of a detail.'[4] For the occasion, Munari made use of beams of polarised light, a technique he had already adopted in the 1950s, and which we shall be discussing later. In conclusion, there was another production in which light played a leading role. In Florence in March 1980, Munari, along with Castiglioni and Mosconi, composed the colour score for Alexander Scriabin's *Prometheus*, the famous symphony that calls for an accompaniment of coloured light linked to the expressive values of the music. The light, or rather its colours, go along with the music, but with a life of their own, avoiding the subordinate role of underlining the musical passage. As on other occasions, Munari spurns synaesthesia, respecting the specific nature of the different means of expression and always avoiding the temptation of symbolism. The experiment is in line with the research carried out by Balla, Ginna and Corra ('chromatic music')

Sketch for *Musical acrobats in cage*, 1935.

Pencil on paper, 1934.

and by Ricciardi and Prampolini ('The stage ... will be ... powerfully enlivened by chromatic emanations of light generated by electric floodlights with multicoloured glass filters').[5]

In the performance there could perhaps be detected a lack of consonance between modern techniques of lighting and the late romantic emphasis of the symphony; it is worth remembering that the music composed in Japan by Toru Takemitsu and in Italy by Luciano Berio was presumably more suited to the spirit of Munari's use of polarised light. In Florence, however, it was the lighting that caught the spectator's interest. Typically in the case of Munari, the light was absolutely natural: the three designers took care to use nothing but light sources (halogen lights, filaments, sodium vapour lamps, wood brands) that had no need of coloured filters. For 19 minutes, there was only the colour of natural light on the stage.

The 1930s also saw Munari developing an interest in industrial design, into whose territory he would venture when the economic and political situation in Italy permitted, i.e. after the war. Undoubtedly influenced by the work of the Bauhaus, and naturally inclined to use the media of art to intervene in daily life, Munari had always shown a propensity to step outside the bounds of the various genres, attempting to hold a dialogue with the public too. As well as working ceramics, which he did in collaboration with the Futurist Tullio d'Albisola — and which he has followed up recently with designs for interior tiling — Munari produced designs for fabrics (winning a prize in 1933), furnishings (in collaboration with Ricas) and interior decorations, taking part in the 1933 Triennial Exhibition in Milan with Prampolini. During this period Munari started to design furniture: photographs still exist of the pieces he produced for his own office and home. They reveal that Munari was more interested in bringing the style of decoration up to date than in reinventing furniture from scratch. In fact his furniture was decorated in the style of his paintings of the time (1935), especially those of the series *The frame too*. Yet the chairs, tables and desks already have clear, simple and definitely modern lines, although one has to wait until after the war to find Munari working as a seasoned designer, with a solid theoretical grounding and perfectly convinced of his own ideas.

The move towards industrial design was also a consummation of his activity as a painter. Munari's paintings had been on show with the Futurists at the exhibitions for the Venice Biennale in 1930 (*Self-portrait, Hand*); in 1932 (*Thicknesses of atmosphere*) and in 1934 (*At the limits of painting, Machines in the wood, Beach*); not in 1936, as is sometimes mistakenly reported. These paintings, of which only the titles remain, caused Antonio Marasco to write, in 1943, that 'Munari's abstraction, like all abstractions, is the totality or the absolute unity of the gamut of sensations'. Hence Munari is an 'eminently

lyrical' artist, who 'uses effective means to achieve the desired portrayal of subjects and objects that have never been seen, but that have been imagined in plastic terms. With objects already stripped of their reality, he invents each time a pictorial or graphic reconstruction that lies completely outside the field of verism or mere naturalism.'[6] Munari as an abstract artist, then, but a Munari who is quoted by Marasco as having written, in 1943, 'I wish to go and see what there is beyond abstract art. Do not believe that one gets over these experiences by turning back.' What led him to this decision?

Over the course of that decade he had experimented with different ways of painting: from the Futurist use of the airbrush to metaphysics and Surrealism, from geometrical abstraction to a sort of organic concretism that reminds one of Hans Arp. He had painted metaphysical landscapes, sought analogies between the mechanical and the organic: in short he had tried almost everything, including photograms, available in that sort of visual laboratory which was a feature of Italy in the 1930s. It took the post-war period to refine these experiences, leading him, for example, no longer to seek analogies between the mechanical and the natural, but to develop the idea of a 'naturalness' inherent in all things.

He also painted the human figure, which interested him, it seems, as a 'machine', but he wrote: 'It should not be thought that human art is that which represents human figures. Euclid's theorem is also human.'[7] Then there was a series of drawings on the theme of the 'easel painter', which was made up of a Futurist self-portrait (1932), a metaphysical one (1937), and then grew simpler, taking on organicist outlines (1938) and finally (1940) becoming abstract in a drawing where forms and structures remain as lines under tension. By dint of pursuing the theme to its very end, it seems that Munari began to lose interest in everything except the internal structure of forms, with the result that, between 1940 and 1943, he produced a number of drawings of lines under tension. These were the prelude to a painting (1943) in which the lines act almost as ties, creating geometric spaces into which the colour is timidly insinuated. It looks almost as if the ground of the picture — as had already happened — was insufficient for the energy of an innovator like Munari. One gets the feeling that, if just one of the lines were to be cut with a razor-blade, the entire painting would shoot out of its frame, creating one of those structures that Munari was to come up with a few years later. It seems that after having experimented with all the ways of structuring and destructuring the picture, Munari wished to move on to something more substantial and more controllable, for him and for the public. Back in 1934 a critic had reported an exchange between Munari and the crowd at an exhibition which gives an indication of the irresistible tendency that had led him towards industrial design:

"'But this is not art and you are not artists!...'' was the

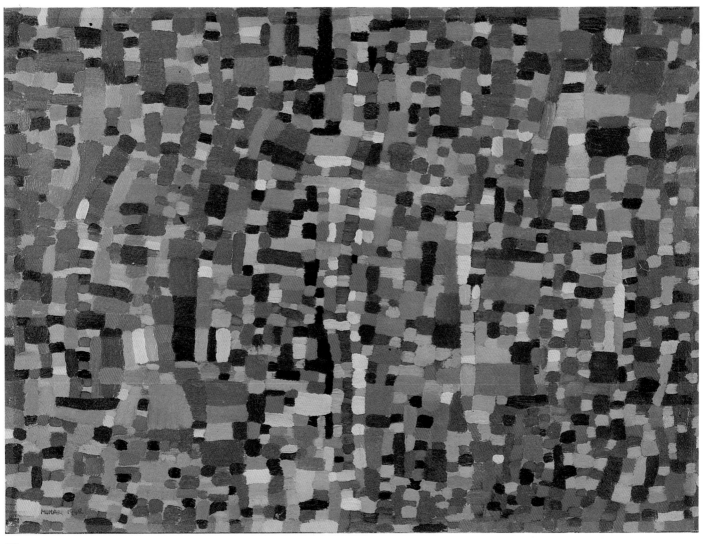

Oil on canvas, 1942.

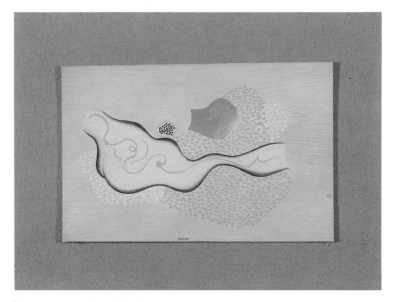

Tempera on paperboard, 1946.

clear-cut conclusion reached by one visitor.
'"What do you mean by artist?'' Munari asked him.
'"Somebody who makes art.''
'"Exactly. Somebody who makes art!... But you, while
protesting about the abuse of the description *artist*, are
always ready, like me, like everyone, to call even your
barber and your shoemaker an *artist*...''
'A chorus of ah!, eh!, oh!, uh!...
'"Don't we tend to say: my barber shaves me like a true
artist!?... my shoemaker is a real artist?... my tailor, what
an artist!?''
'"So we need to find a word to replace that of *artist*,''
chimed in an ironic and unidentifiable voice from the
crowd.'[8]
'Artists ought to take an interest in machines ... they
should start to learn about mechanical anatomy, mechanical
language, to understand the nature of machines, *to strain
them by making them function in an irregular fashion*, to
create works of art with the machines themselves, with
their very means.'[9] This was in 1938. Munari, heir of
Futurism, refused to go on glorifying the machine: he
preferred getting to know it and using it. In this he was
faithful to his own principle of trying to do something
different with an object that is generally always used or
experienced in the same way. Moreover, he was getting
interested again in making machines 'useless': his later
research to which he gave the name *Arhythmic machine*
(1951), was connected with the observation of energies
'that are released by regular and rhythmically functioning
mechanisms' and that serve to maintain 'regular mechanical
running, discharging excessive energy from the machine. In
my research into arhythmia, on the other hand, I sought to
make this energy, which could be described as fortuitous,
act by encouraging arhythmic movements... so as to make
the functioning of a machine less regular, especially if its
functioning is totally useless and unproductive.'[10] Here,
then, there is a planned, rational and exact side — and its
polemical, fortuitous and Dada counterpart. Enrico Bay has
written that Munari designs machines that function, like
our hearts, when they are subject to emotion. From the
Futurist idea, one of Marinetti's, of the analogy between
man and machine, Munari came to the conclusion that it
was right to endow the machine with emotions and
feelings, so that we ourselves, instead of becoming
mechanised, rediscover with them the joy of contemplation.
Munari's attitude falls somewhere between that of Dada
and that of Zen. If Dada represents his love for
fortuitousness — a love which led him to investigate the
laws of chance, or the planning of chance — it is
nevertheless bound up with a view of the world similar to
the acceptance of opposites in Zen. Just look at some of
the titles of his works: *Unreadable books, Travelling
sculptures, Fossils of the year 2000, Reconstructions of
imaginary objects, Original xerographs, Negative positives,
Concave convexes, Useless machines* and so on. The regular
must be accompanied by the irregular, the plan by
accident, the productive by the useless, just like day and

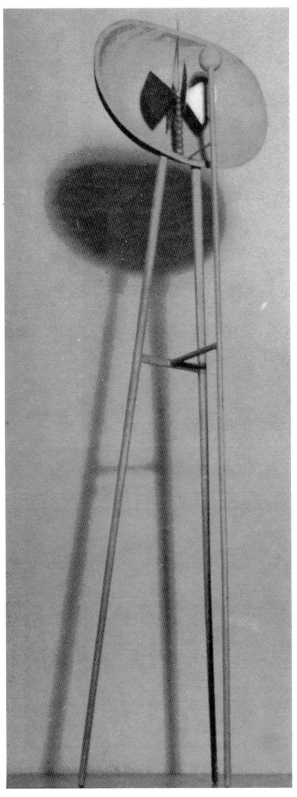

Useless machine, painted wood, 1933.

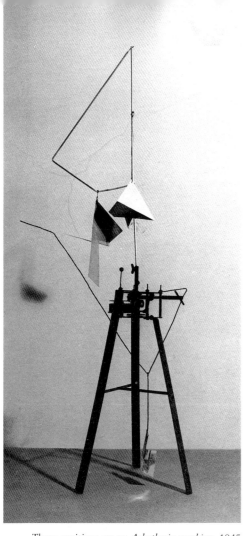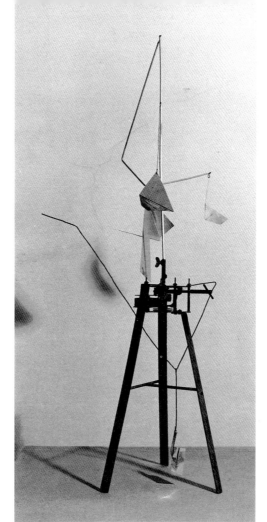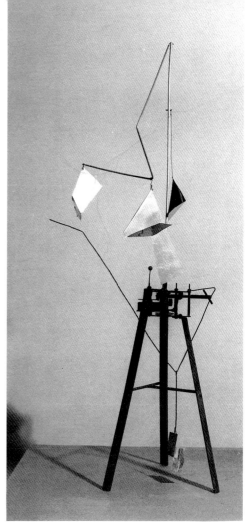

Three positions on an *Arhythmic machine*, 1945.

Useless machine, painted wood, 1933.

night, man and woman, hot and cold. As Menna has pointed out, in the geography of contemporary art Munari maintains 'an attitude in which the exclusive fervour of the Futurists appears to be lightened by a playful component that seems to derive from the abstract metaphysical irony of Duchamp: between the wholly positive approach of the former and the extreme negation of the latter, Munari seeks in fact to establish a new equilibrium, in which the opposing tendencies are taken up together, but liberated from their extreme aspects and brought together in a new dialectical relationship of acceptance and irony, of gravity and playfulness, of "positive and negative"'.[11]

So Munari brought the irregular into machines. But in that 'machine' or 'system' that is Munari's world, where every single work refers to all the others, what is the relay that closes the system's circuit, connecting the positive pole of the useful to the negative one of the useless? Irony. Irony circulates always and everywhere in Munari's world. For it has a very important function. It is not an accidental, personal irony, but a methodical one, which helps Munari to check each of his designs, each of his statements, each of his works. All that he does, says or writes is brushed

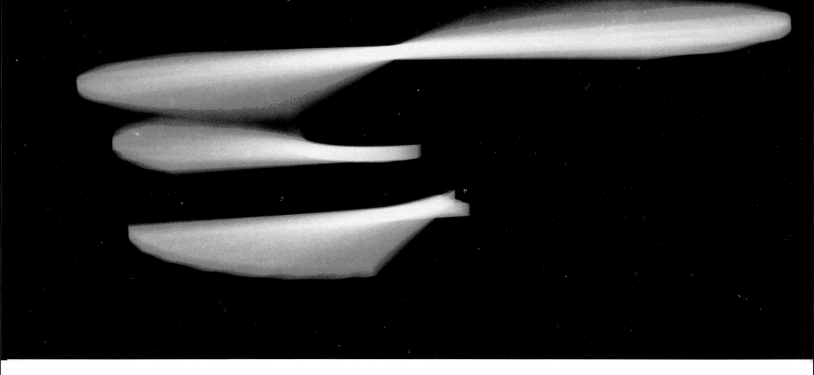

the wrong way by a joke or a gesture that says completely
the opposite of what the artist had been claiming up till
then. The irony contradicts it, but at the same time it
completes it. It is the complement to his action. It is like
the uselessness of his machines. It is the irregularity in his
level, positive discussion of art. It is disorder as opposed to
order. It is doubt about certainty. It is the gift of ubiquity.
If for Munari, as for the ancient Chinese, the only
constant in reality is movement, then irony is movement
too: 'knowing that a thing can be something else is a type
of knowledge connected with mutation. Mutation is the
only constant in reality.' For this reason, processes or
assertions in which Munari has apparently reached a
conclusion are suddenly set in motion again by an
invention, a joke or a pun that makes one laugh and think.
Irony is always an invitation to go further, to ignore the
hypothesis of a definitive and final result: for this is
transformation, temporality, the fourth dimension. In the
'Munari machine' irony is the spark that gets the motor
going again. Which permits Munari to avoid himself and
his research being consigned to a museum. Irony as

stimulus, as counterweight, investigation and verification of
the balance achieved. In Zen practice, this corresponds to
the blow inflicted on the pupil by his master, not as
punishment but to bring him back to reality, to draw him
away from abstract thought and get his feet back on the
ground. So irony is also the intervention of chance, just as
in nature the force of the wind compels the tree to assume
an unexpected shape. Irony is, along with the quest for
essentiality, a constant feature of Munari's sixty years of
art and creativity. The difficulty of fitting Munari into
chronological categories tells us a lot about the validity of
the argument put forward by a variety of critics: that
Munari represents a world, a system that is always in
dynamic equilibrium between pairs of complementary
opposites.
The distinctive features of Munari's work were already
present in the 1930s. Some in embryo, others fully
developed in the artist's consciousness. It should be noted
that Munari has always kept in close contact with all the
artistic developments of his time. But although it is easy
to find a dense web of references, influences and links with

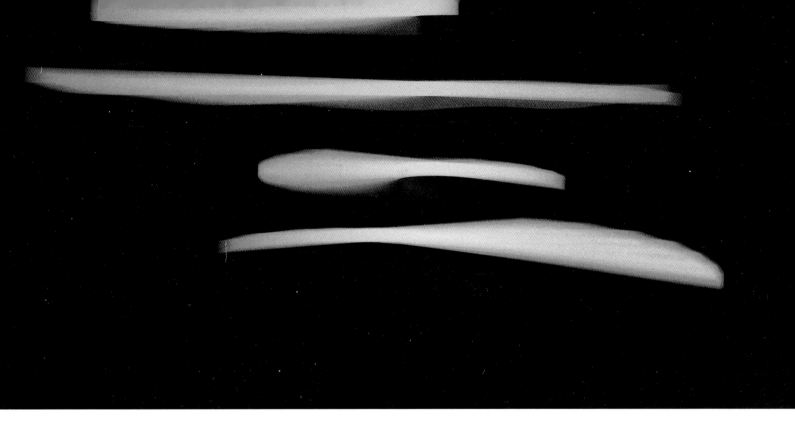

Useless machine, in movement, white wood with coloured sections, 1947.

Design for *Useless machine no. 77*, to be made out of painted wood, 1939.

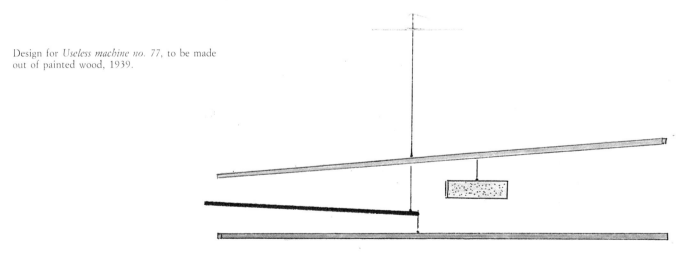

The *Useless machines*, first produced in 1933, are even today the series of objects most characteristic of Munari. Receiving a cool reception at first, they represented one of the first examples of kinetic art and one of the earliest attempts to move away from the static nature of abstract art, by setting geometric forms free in space. The idea of the machine was already accompanied by the concept of uselessness, and by inference the unproductiveness of much human and mechanical activity, a concept to which Munari drew attention well ahead of his contemporaries.

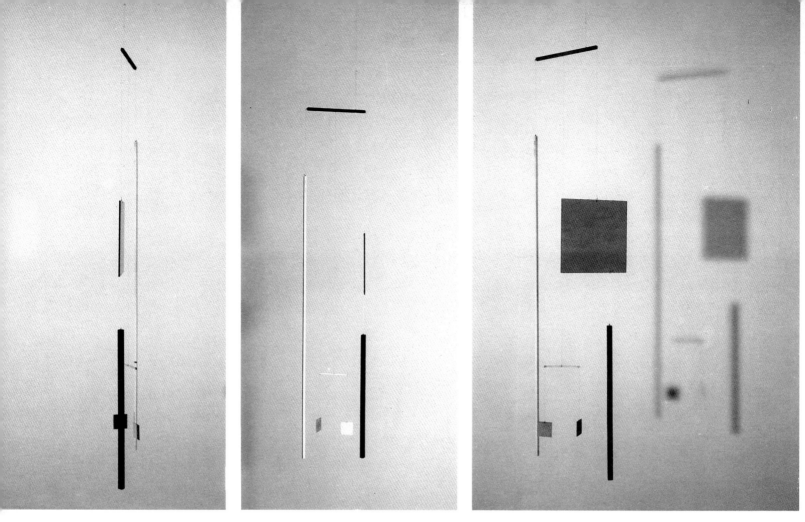

Three positions of a *Useless machine* made out of wood, perspex and metal, 1949.

artists and movements, it is difficult to detect affinities profound enough to categorise Munari as belonging to any one of them. For it seems that Munari always tends to absorb influences and suggestions, making them part of his own system of producing art, within his own conception of the world. The lines along which he worked were often personal interpretations of motifs to be found in avant-garde movements. This does not mean that he was never a Futurist, a metaphysician, an abstractionist, etc. Nor that he has not been, or is not, a Dadaist as well. Once again, let us return to the 1950s: 'Take several pieces of black, coloured or wrapping paper ... anything that comes to hand; break one of these in two or three pieces and let them fall onto a sheet of drawing paper. Do the same thing

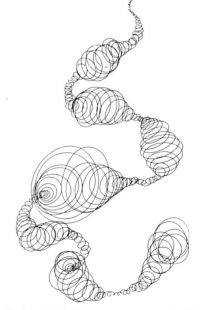

Birobotanics, ball-point pen on paper, 1950.

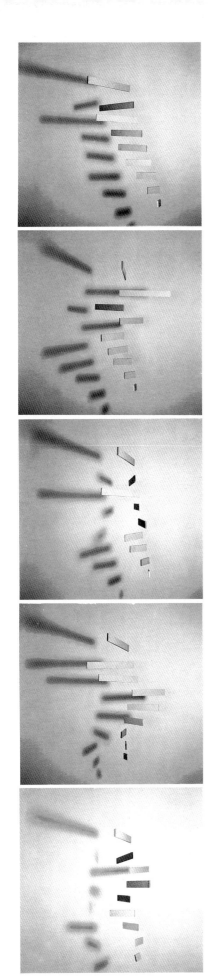

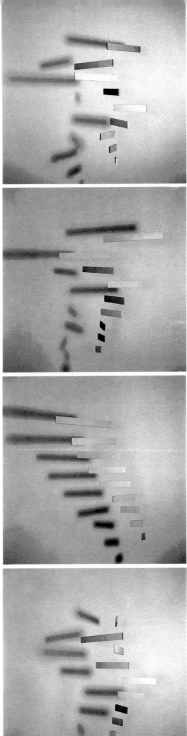

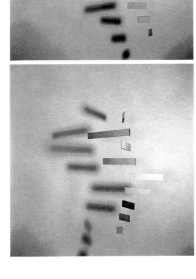

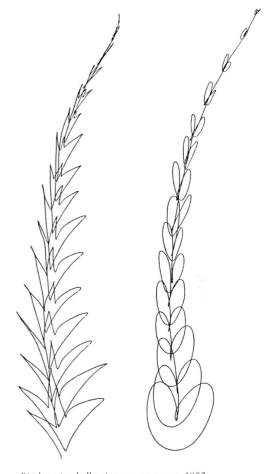

Birobotanics, ball-point pen on paper, 1952.

39

Useless machine in movement, wood with coloured sections, 1947.

Birobotanics, ball-point
pen on paper, 1952.

Munari at work in his spare time.

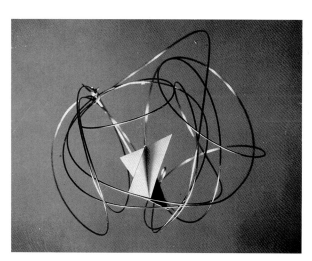

Useless machine no. 75, steel wire, 1947.

Few have accepted technology and the world of the
machine as serenely as Munari; and even fewer have been
able to introduce 'into this enthusiastic acceptance an
element of carelessness with regard to pure functionality,
in such a way as to place the accent on the component of
a free and joyful contemplation-enjoyment of the object'
(Menna). His *Arhythmic machines* constrain the machine
to 'useless', unproductive and non-economic gestures. On
the one hand a sort of Futurist activism; on the other a
notion of 'waste' highly familiar to the European culture
of this century. However, Munari never accentuates such
contrasts, preferring results that are aesthetically
significant but trivial to those that are dramatic.

One of the first *Useless machines*, at rest and
in movement, 1951, Krefeld museum.

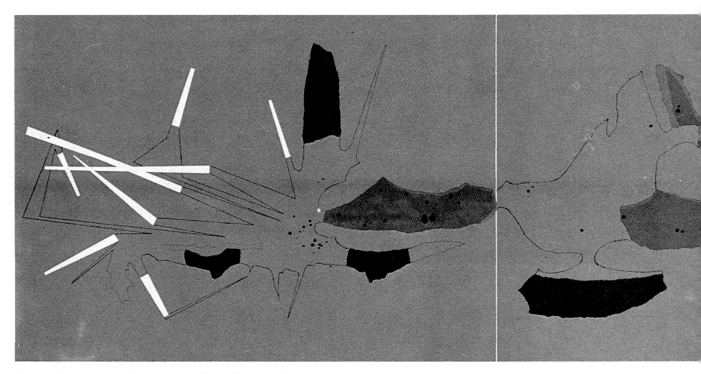

Theoretical reconstruction of an imaginary object, collage and drawing, 1960.

with a different piece of paper. The objects (fragments) dropped onto the sheet in this way will take up a haphazard position. Examine this pattern and, after long observation, it may be that something needs to be shifted, but not for a logical reason, according to a rule. Rather according to "the rule of chance" as Hans Arp puts it. Something has to be "felt" which "makes the hand move".'

These are the instructions which Munari — always generous with information about his methods — gave and followed for his *Theoretical reconstructions of imaginary objects* (1959). But, peering out of this Dada situation, one can find Munari's concern with design, which leads him to remobilise, to give order to the poetics of chance: 'Well, having made any such shifts, one begins to link up the various pieces. To do this one must look at the outlines of the fragments and their internal structure; if a piece is torn it has a different edge to one that is cut and connections between torn pieces will follow the shape of the tear and those between cut pieces will be rectilinear. Music paper has the lines of the stave and notes which, one supposes, will behave like the threads of a torn piece of cloth, but with rigidity.'[12]

There is thus an aspect of visual contemplation alongside a mental and conceptual one in Munari's work. For this reason it seems right to insist, as Menna did in 1966, on the parallel with Marcel Duchamp. They have interest in common, and similar paradoxical assumptions: 'the warm side of geometry' in Munari; Duchamp's 'units of measure' or 'entertaining physics'. The quest for ambiguity in language (Munari: *'il nullatenente non era nemmeno sufficiente'*, 'Bernard the Great was born astride two centuries. His mother suffered greatly'; Duchamp: *'Un mot de Reine; des maux de reins'*). Both put forward a topology of their own, which was 'geometry on a sheet of rubber', where no rigid bodies existed and everything could change in size, shape and position. Finally, and once again, the machine. 'The French artist sets out to demystify and satirise the machine but ends up, in fact, by raising it for the first time to the status of the subject of a work of art; Munari on the other hand, starts out from a typically Futurist acceptance of the world of technology and machines, but he introduces into this fervent assent an element of distraction with regard to pure functionality, so as to place the accent on a free and joyful contemplation and utilisation of the object' (Menna).[13]

Munari is one of the most prolific writers among contemporary artists. Books, articles, features, introductions to his own works, artistic manifestos: all are symptomatic of his desire to communicate, to explain everything that, in

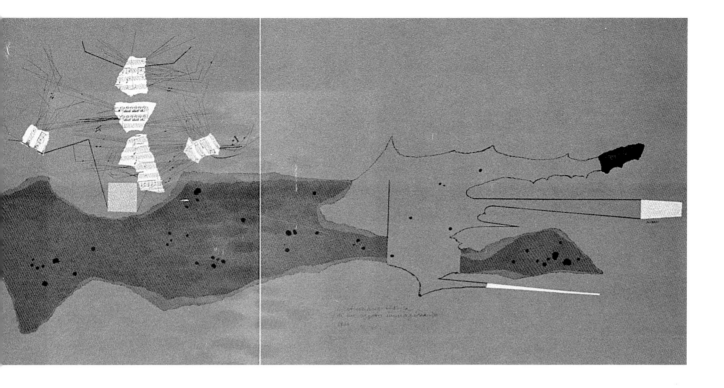

visual communication, can be explained. His ability to write with clarity and simplicity derives from a moral and civic committment: participation in the life of all men and the intention to change it for the better with the instruments of the visual operator. He knows how to be irreverent, always for the same ends. He can be ironic and poke fun at himself for — as has already been pointed out — irony is ingrained in his way of seeing and living in the world. He knows how to rejuvenate great literary traditions like the *pastiche* (which has always been very popular in Lombardy) by means of rhetorical devices such as accumulation, enumeration and paronymy. It suffices to read ironic passages like the following, describing the properties of an armchair: 'Stuffed, covered with fabric, fur, natural or dyed leather, vinilup, sevenua, lax and tex, plush, velvet, velveteens, cotton, straw, travertine, nylon, orlon, filon, cordon or burlon'.[14]

Or to put out 'nonsense' in the manner of Campanile or Allais: a coolly prepared and planned nonsense. A number of his works would lose a great deal if they were not accompanied by his presentations, where moral entreaties or technical descriptions are counterbalanced by remarks that give an edge, an ironic stimulus which completes the design by keeping it open. He is always coming up with delightful plays on words that he defines as 'semantic disturbances'. He also composed, during the 1940s, a number of interesting poems of art, often with a sententious, gnomic tone. Somewhere between the enunciated and the lyrical, they have taken the name of *Theorems*. Munari has written and is still writing a great deal because he feels the urge to communicate his way of making and perceiving art without intercession. For him, the public is not made up solely of 'authorised persons', as he makes clear in his delightful preface to the book *Le macchine di Munari* (1942):

'Entrance is forbidden to those not employed on works
'Work is forbidden to those not intended for entrance
'The person involved with those not forbidden to work has grown fat
'The chalk is washed for those not involved in wholesale...
'Entrance is forbidden to those employed on works.'[15]

After all, Munari's relations with art critics have not always been idyllic: Munari has often picked them as a target for his scintillating prose, taking off a number of critical categories with exhilarating results that are reminiscent of Woody Allen:

The hermetic critic
So the art of this artist is not a common 'art', nor is it an ordinary *art*; it is Art, in fact (art) understood as art.

The enquiring critic
But who does this artist think he is? A misunderstood genius? How can he believe that what he does should be regarded as art by right-minded people? And what kind of art? And why does he paint with the handle of the brush? Doesn't he know that the bristles are on the other end? Who does he expect to understand it? And then, when all is said and done, let us be frank about it: is this stuff art? Where are we going to end up? And then?

The highly erudite critic
The gnoseological aspect of the hedone that the onlooker perceives from the holistic structures is diachronically biased towards the Kitsch. The epistructures of the continuum, on the other hand, incorporate a proairetic quotient with reiterable feed-back. The phantom appearance and iconicity of the patterns are the atomistic, but obsolete, elements of deontology for a reclamation of the utilitas.[16]

Tempera on paper, 1949.

The cat Meo, toy made out of reinforced foam-rubber, capable of taking any shape, 1952.

Tempera on paper, 1947.

Design for a cover of *La lettura*, tempera on paper, 1945.

Another important line of research, among the many
pursued by Munari, was one that extended over a span of
more than twenty years: a series of temperas on paper or
canvas, *taches* produced by light brush-strokes, also
present in his airbrush paintings of the 1920s (the
inspiration came from Herbert Bayer, probably
responsible for much of Munari's Surrealism as well). The
taches are evidence — even when they take on decidedly
abstract forms — of an interest in natural phenomena,
such as the reflections of light on water.

Munari's forks, bent forks, 1958.

Munari's Machines, a book written and illustrated in its entirety by Munari, contains imaginary and comic machines, inspired by those of Rube Goldberg. The latter, a famous American caricaturist, also contributed to *New York Dada*, the review founded by Marcel Duchamp in the 1920s. In the book we find an interplay between design and the nonsense so typical of Munari. Descriptions and drawings are provided of machines such as the 'Tail wagger for lazy dogs', the 'Machine for training alarm-clocks', the 'Lizard motor for tired tortoises', the 'Sprinkling device for making hiccups musical' (which looks like the opposite of his *Arhythmics*), etc.

Here one can detect his affection for writers like the great Alphonse Allais, whose main character, Captain Cap, boasted of holding the world record for the millimetre, on track and road. It is enough to read Munari's wonderful accounts of the invention of the cigarette or the handshake to realise that Italy has here a comic writer on a par with the best of Campanile or the great Petrolini (in fact one seems to hear Petrolini's voice in some of Munari's questions and answers: 'Do you know why, in churches, the organ is always very large? Because the organ is used for functions in churches. And, as is well known, function develops the organ').

At other times Munari's typewriter takes on artists or established art movements, like Pop art or Nouveau réalisme: 'How on earth does our age produce such works of art? ... A transparent box full of used dentures. Shit in a tin, signed by the author, 10 ½-kilo tins; a show window dummy painted white, a cloth parcel with a hundred thousand fastenings made out of different kinds of string. A machine that draws doodles; a picture made by reversing its colours at random. A 12-metre-long tube of toothpaste.' Or his target might be the social realism of the 1950s: '... A very large painting of social protest where one sees poverty-stricken peasants trampled beneath capitalist boots (a highly expensive painting suitable only for purchase by capitalists for the drawing-room of their villa in Varese)'.[17]

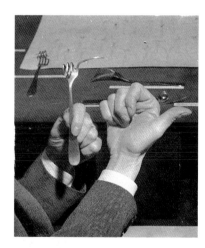

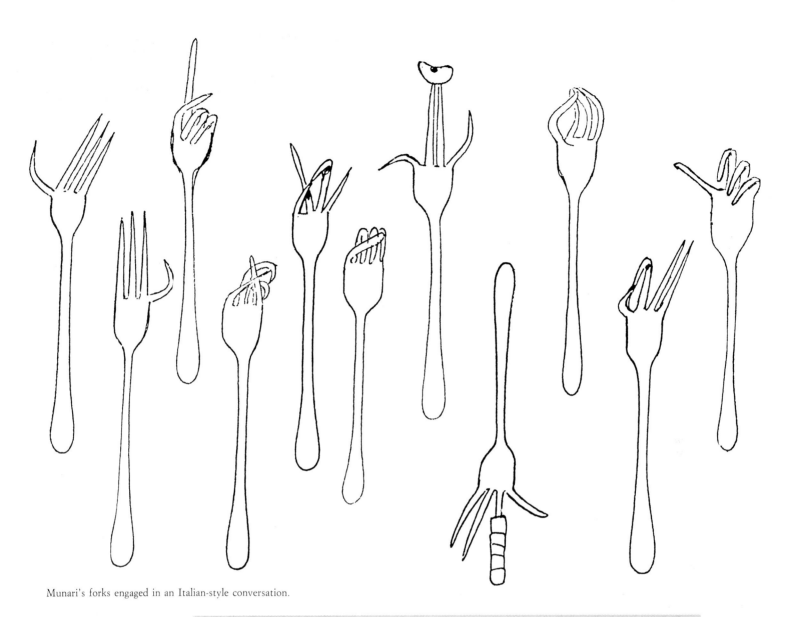

Munari's forks engaged in an Italian-style conversation.

Indecipherable script of an unknown people, 1972, Risari collection.

Eyeshades, 1953. Published in *Stildomus* in 1955, they were later used, without their creator's knowledge, during the American presidential elections by 'Ike' Eisenhower.

Eisenhower with the *Eyeshades*.

The first carpet with a mutable pattern, 1986. Prod. Sisal. The black marks change position as the carpet is walked on.

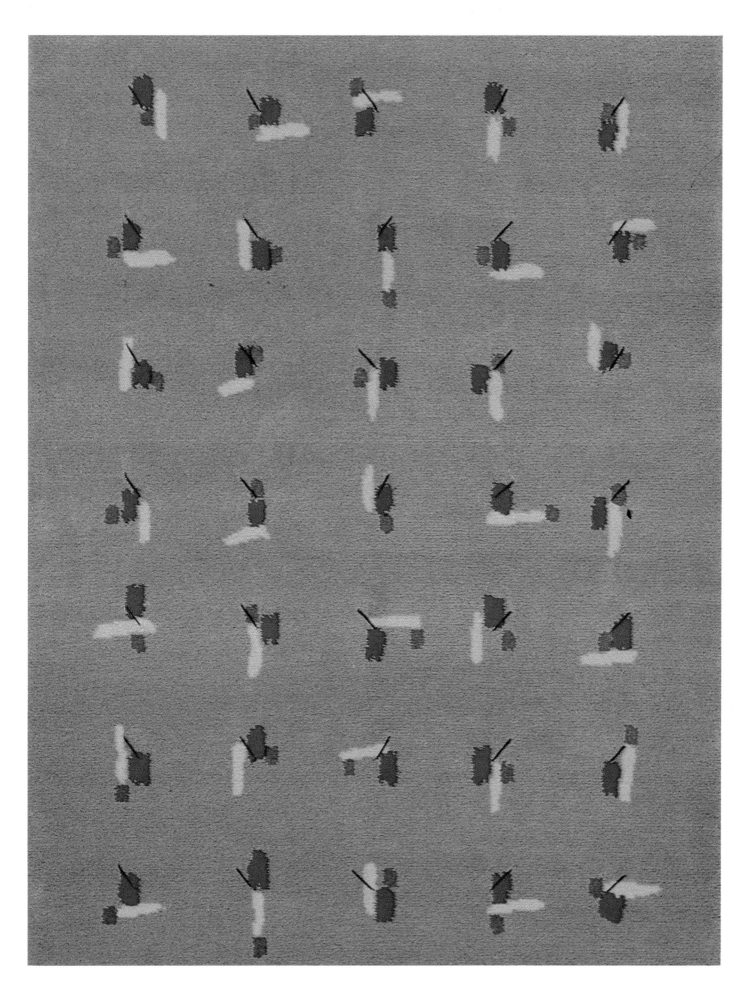

When he returned to Badia Polesine on holiday, Munari took souvenir photographs of parents and friends, 1935.

Books like *Fotocronache*, from 1940, bear witness to Munari's inclination to meddle in everything, even writing. In *Fotocronache*, comic passages, nonsense, photomontages, paradoxical critical comments on art, a rigorous and unusual make-up, everything is by Munari, ready as graphic artist, painter, sculptor, designer — and writer too — to participate in the atmosphere of post-war reconstruction. A reconstruction that for Munari — and not for him alone — signified a search for new directions in art and communication.

Cartoon, pencil on paper, 1930.

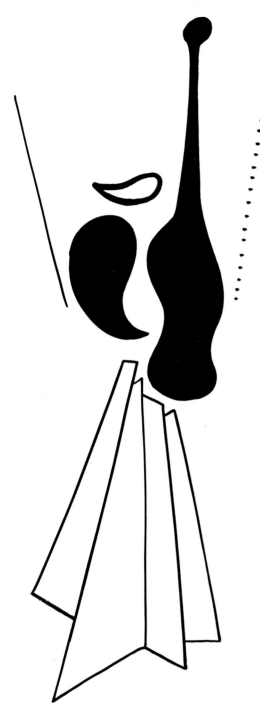

Painter at the easel, Indian ink on paper, 1940.

'Any shop in a large modern city, with its elegant windows in which useful and delightful objects are on display, gives more artistic pleasure than all the vaunted traditionalist exhibitions.' Thus wrote Balla in 1918: words that find a significant parallel in a series of articles and gnomic poems by Munari, published in *AZ* in the first few months of 1950.
In them Munari clarified his definitive move into the realms of industrial design, claiming that it was the duty of the artist to play an active, professional role in satisfying the requirements of industrial civilisation.

Art as profession

During the second world war Munari, rejected as medically unfit for military service, was nevertheless sent for a while to serve with an anti-aircraft battery; ironically, the battery was completely without shells. From 1939 to 1943, however, he worked as a graphic artist for a newspaper controlled by the regime, alongside a future Nobel prize-winner, the poet Salvatore Quasimodo. 'Munari used to wait for us in his rather secluded art director's office,' Arturo Tofanelli recalls today. 'He rapidly made up the texts and photographs that we brought him without ever discussing their merits. There was nothing on his walls to remind you of the war, just his own things: abstract compositions, drawings.'[1] After the upheaval of the war, right away we come across a work by Munari with an emblematic title: *X hour*. This was an ordinary alarm-clock, whose spring-driven mechanism was used by Munari to turn three half-discs. The discs were in the primary colours, but transparent, so that they produced other colours and shapes as they were superimposed. It was a kinetic object — the first to be subsequently mass-produced, in 1963 — obtained by 'making useless' a mechanism designed for other purposes. Its title, even if only by coincidence, seems to be warning us that something was changing in Munari's art: it was the hour of design and programmed art.

In the immediate post-war period Milan was the main centre for the earliest manifestations of concrete art. It was principally Swiss concrete artists, such as Max Huber and Max Bill, who got in touch with the most talented Italian artists, resulting in the organisation of a major exhibition of concrete art in 1947. Works by artists including Klee, Kandinsky, Arp, Lohse, Herbin and Bill were put on show alongside those of the Italians Licini, Mazzon, Veronesi, Rho, Sottsass Jr., Munari and many others. The following year Soldati, Munari, Dorfles and Monnet founded the Movimento Arte Concreta. Within a short period, it had brought together the best of the Italian concretists. The MAC attempted to establish links with the experiments in concrete art that had been carried out before the war, but it had been set up in an extremely hostile environment: the artistic milieu in Italy suffered from a dearth of international connections, lagging behind post-Cubist developments or getting bogged down in the themes of social realism while the critics turned their attention to pre-war trends such as 'Chiarismo lombardo'. The history of the MAC is still a disputed one, shot through with disagreements, splits and misunderstandings, while it is clear that the group totally lacked a solid theoretical basis. An attempt was made to revive the concept of a 'synthesis of the arts' in terms of a rationalist culture, but over the course of the ten years that the movement lasted the effort to reconcile architecture, industrial design and the visual arts failed to produce significant results. Munari played an important part in these events, and was elected president of the MAC in 1953.

Curved negative positive, oil on board, 1951.

X hour, first motor-driven multiple, 1945.
Mass-produced by Danese in 1963.

BERTINI   MUNARI   GIULIA SALA   DI SALVATORE   SALTO   DORFLES   SALTO JR.   REGINA   MAZZON   VERONESI

Group photograph of some of the members of the MAC (Concrete Art Movement) at the Salto bookshop in Milan, c. 1950.

In catalogue number 10 of the MAC, devoted to the exhibition 'Mechanisation disintegralism total art organic art public danger', the *Manifesto of Mechanisation* drawn up by Munari in 1938 was also published. Balla and the Futurists were mentioned in the editorial and one can detect the hand of Munari, especially in passages like the following:

'How can one expect today's public still to take an interest in the problems of painting or sculpture when it is accustomed to seeing everything resolved in concrete terms in the cinema, in illuminated advertising, in the great three-dimensional publicity signs of the international fairs... So is art dead or has it just altered aspect without many people noticing? What would Leonardo be doing today: the Montecatini pavilion or an oil-on-canvas portrait of Miss Europe? Art is not dead, it has merely altered course and this is where we must look for it. It no longer responds to the old.'[2]

Hence it was neither a question of changing the way of painting, nor of bringing Italian artistic culture up to date, but of making a decisive shift towards real life.

Munari's experience in the MAC — which came to an end in 1958 — did not just mean getting involved in industrial design, but also a parallel involvement in a mathematical approach to art. After pre-war experiences in Europe like those of De Stijl, a large group of artists — including a few veterans of the Bauhaus, among them Albers and Bill — tried to achieve maximum objectivity in the realisation of works of art, seeking to construct an autonomous and specific language in painting and sculpture. Munari

belonged to this group, as is demonstrated by later experiments such as the *Relationships between the forms of Peano* (1974) but even more by the series of *Sequences* dating from the early 1950s. This was a series of spots of colour made to rotate on the surface of the paper in a precise pattern. Along with these came the series of *Negative positives*, in which Munari sought to free the painting of all its non-objective elements, returning to his reflections on the problem of ground in abstract pictures. Each element of the *Negative positives* can be considered both as foreground and as background, as far as its optical effect is concerned, but no part of the picture is a static ground: each shape advances or recedes, creating a chromatic dynamism, a continuously threatened equilibrium. As Paolo Fossati has pointed out, the old theme of the ambiguity of forms is no longer there. Instead one finds a combination of continuously shifting points of view. Then in a number of the *Negative positives* gaps were left so that the wall could form part of the composition. But Munari did not cease to pursue other lines of experimentation in his painting during those years: just as the *Negative positives* have their roots in the series *The frame too*, *A blue point*, a painting he produced in 1937, seems to be the starting-point for temperas like *Archipelago* (1948), a composition of brush-strokes that also recalls some of his work from the beginning of the 1930s. Some other tempera and oil paintings, still Futurist in style, also seem to hark back to Prampolini, while others achieve a surprising degree of chromatic intensity, obtained by means of small *taches* or brush-strokes that render the surface of the picture perceptibly dynamic, and that seem to derive

Structure under tension, wood and string, 1948.

The first *Negative positive*, oil on board, 1950.

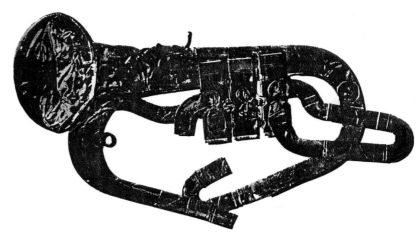

Bugle of peace, squashed bugle, 1950.

In 1948 a group of artists set up the MAC, which organised a number of important exhibitions and enlivened modern Italian art with its activism in the Futurist mould, fighting a disorderly battle on behalf of concrete art.

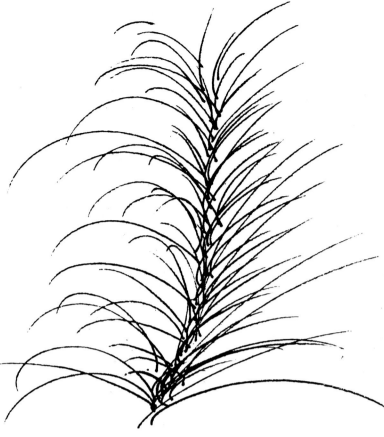

Pencil on paper, 1945.

Tempera on paperboard, 1948.

Tempera on paper, 1950.

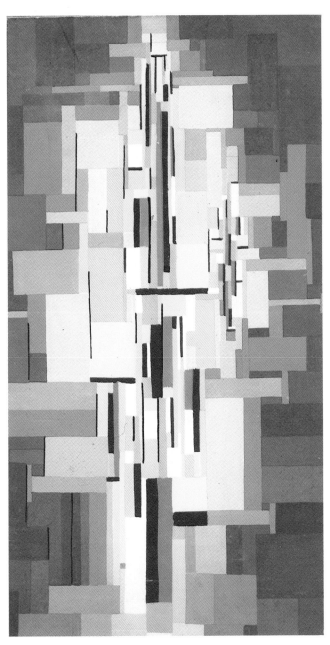

Tempera on paperboard, 1948.

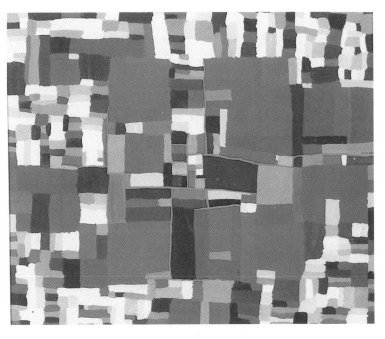

Tempera on paperboard, 1945.

Sketches for the first *Negative positives*, 1950.

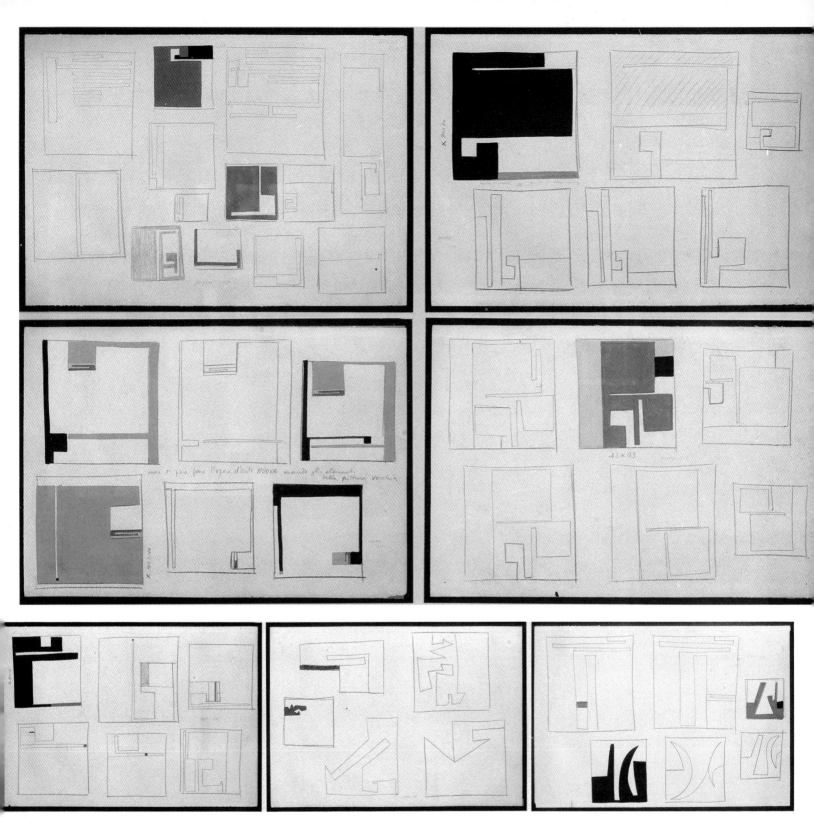

Some of the 500 sketches for the *Negative positives*. From the early sketches, still confined to the area of the picture, Munari moved on to *Negative positives* of different shapes, where the colour of the wall becomes part of the composition.

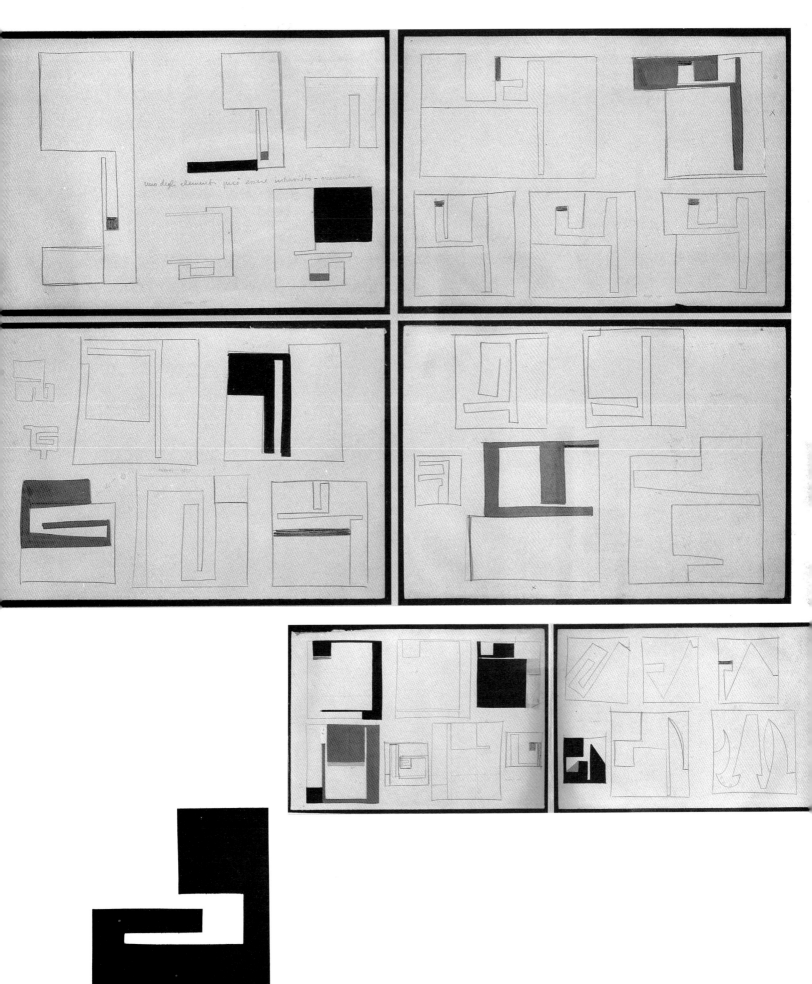

In the early 1950s, after he had come into contact with Gestalt theories, Munari tackled the theme of optical perception in his series of *Negative positives*. In these each element of the picture can be regarded either as background or as foreground. The effect obtained is that of a perceptual restlessness; yet it is a restlessness that generates not ambiguity, but contiguity, adjacency. It is another response, following that of the *Useless machines*, to the problem of 'ground', which for Munari was always akin to useless background noise, and therefore inessential.

Curved negative positive, oil on canvas, 1951.

Negative positive, acrylic on canvas, 1951.

Illustrations from *Fotocronache*, 1942.

Negative positive, acrylic on canvas, 1978.

from Balla's work. A series of 32 preparatory sketches for paintings took yet another direction: forms laid out horizontally and vertically as in one of Mondrian's pictures, but they are 'degenerate', expanded forms, almost a critical homage paid to the Dutch master.

From the early 1950s onwards, interludes began to appear in Munari's work as a painter. These were filled not only by industrial design, but also by programmed art and the expectation of a new encounter with the public through mass-produced art objects.

More recently, Munari has carried out a conceptual operation involving painting in *Oil on canvas* (1980). Various rough canvases made of vegetable fibre (linen, hemp, cotton, etc.) were stippled with vegetable oil, extracted from the seeds of linen, hemp, etc. Munari is again mocking academic art by painting — after all these years — pictures in oil on canvas. But it is a gentle mockery, pointing its finger at the naturalness of paintings that recreate a vegetal situation in an art gallery.

In 1952 Munari had also tried to paint with light: using a polarising filter, he projected fascinating patterns of light that were produced by a very simple procedure. In fact all that the *Projections of polarised light* required were some pieces of cellophane, a polarising filter, slide-frames and a projector: the idea was to bring a collection of miniaturised art into every home. Munari went on to make an experimental film, *The colours of light*, in which his *Projections* were used. His *Projections of direct light* were produced not long before these. A variety of materials were set in slide-frames and projected, thereby revealing their structure. Some of these materials, however, were not put together at random but in carefully arranged compositions, achieving a high level of formal organisation even though they were only a few square centimetres in size.

His involvement with the MAC was decisive for Munari. If he had laid the foundations for a conception of art open to the public in the 1930s, it was his experience in the MAC and the emerging field of Italian design that completed the process, moving him towards an art *by* everybody, and not *for* everybody, as he has gone out of his way to emphasise recently. An article written in 1950 has what sounds like a programmatic title: art is a trade.

'Today the public demands a fine advertising poster, a cover for a book, the decoration of a store, colours for the home, the shape of an iron or of a sewing-machine.

'Think how much there is to do, how many objects, how many things are awaiting the artist's intervention. Go out of the studio and look at the streets too, how many clashing colours, how many shop windows that could look better, how many signs in bad taste, how many badly-done three-dimensional forms. Why not do something? Why not help to improve the appearance of the world in which we live along with a public that does not understand us and does not know what to do with our art?'[3]

Direct projections, materials inserted between glass slides and projected, 1953.

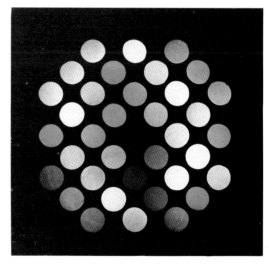

Polariscope, 1953. One of the first works using polarised light, by means of which the colours of the light were continually appearing and changing.

After 1960 Munari extended his concept of 'everybody's art' (as opposed to that of 'art for everybody') to embrace an attempt to preserve the freedom and creativity of children by means of actions, interventions and demonstrations.

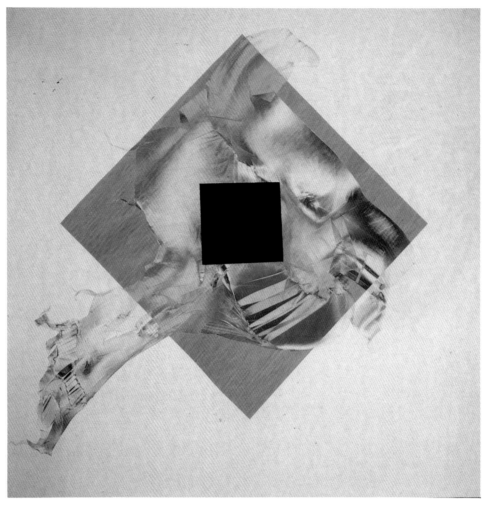

Composition with polarised light, 1953.

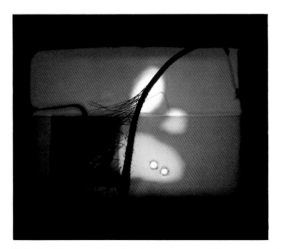 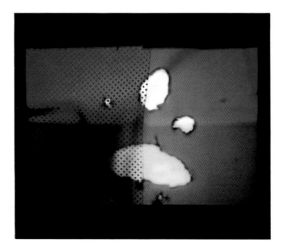

Slide for *Direct multifocal projections* at two different
moments. The image changes by varying the focal depth,
1950.

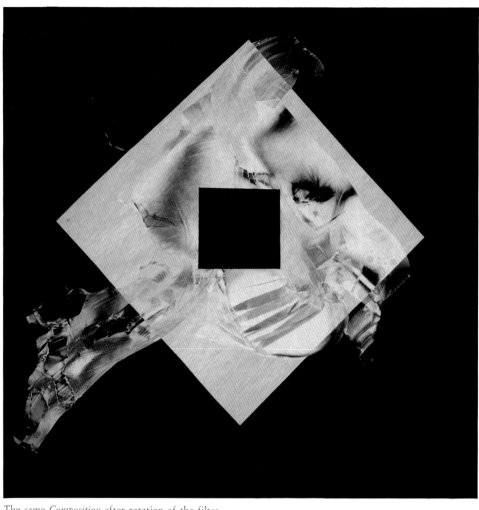

The same *Composition* after rotation of the filter.

Children in the infants' workshop in Tokyo.

In his quest for new materials to be used for aesthetic purposes, Munari came across polaroid, a filter that polarises light, breaking it down into the colours of the spectrum. A piece of transparent plastic, set between two polaroid slides and projected, reveals the colours of light in accordance with the way in which it has been bent or stretched. If the polarising filter is then rotated, the colours run through all shades of the spectrum. For the first time a composition had been obtained through a process of decomposition.

Munari puts his passion for materials at the disposal of a scheme for reconstruction of the universe, without artistic conditions, constantly seeking the essential in all things. A reconstruction that has Futurist roots, although biased in a functionalist direction and passed through the filter of irony. As Andrea Branzi has pointed out recently, the phenomenon of Italian design was only able to emerge thanks to the rationalist requirements present in Futurism. Munari the designer is not rigidly separate from Munari the artist. This is because he has introduced the concept of 'useless' and 'unproductive' into design, and also because his experience with design has led him into lines of artistic research involving mathematical or at any rate rational instruments. His devotion to nature has brought him round to the idea of 'industrial naturalness': 'The final form of these objects has the naturalness of things produced by nature herself. This is the imitation of nature...: imitation of systems of construction and not of finished forms'.[4] Among his most famous productions, there is one that directly exemplifies this concept of invented nature, structured in the same way as the nature with which we are familiar: the knitted lamp. Formed simply out of a tube of synthetic and elastic knitwear and a number of iron rings, the lamp spontaneously assumes a shape of its own. This shape is reminiscent of the bamboo, not because it is an imitation, but because of its inherent structural and formal coherence; this is obtained through the use of a module, the behaviour of the materials and the weight of the lamp itself, which causes it to lengthen into its final shape.

Another aspect of the rapport between design and nature in Munari is shown us by the *Continuous structures* (1961), an object with an 'aesthetic function', made up of interlocking metal elements which can be combined by the user in a variety of ways. In his presentation of the object, Munari draws attention to the factor of chance which can introduce unforeseeable changes into the design, whether in the natural or the artificial world:
'In nature we find continuous structures of various kinds
it may be interesting to try and understand
this aspect of nature
how these structures are formed
how they grow how they are deformed
since an element of chance not yet clearly ascertained
modifies these structures whilst they are formed.'[5]
The *Continuous structures*, alterable at will, appertain to a dynamic conception of art, subject to chance transformations, deliberately designed to change with time and not to survive it. Hence each structure will be different from the others, but all will resemble one another.

Munari with his wife in a photograph taken by Ugo Mulas, 1955.

Indian ink on paper, 1945.

There is a continual dialogue, in Munari's objects, between fixed, classical forms and forms in continuous mutation. Just as the wind can change the shape of trees, continuous use of some objects alters their form. The designer has to take this into account, Munari points out, in confirmation of his interest in the temporal category. All his objects are devised in the simplest way possible, answering both to a requirement of design and to a desire for clarity: 'It is always a question of clarity, of simplicity. There is much work to do that involves taking away, instead of adding. Taking away the superfluous in order to give exact information, instead of adding to and complicating the information.'[6]

His lamps, for instance, can all be folded up into two dimensions; his ashtrays are obtained through an indispensable minimum of folding. Through the use of a module he produces shapes with a formal coherence, but Munari is never in search of pure forms and the total lack of applied decoration is merely the outcome of his quest for essentiality. This does not mean that he neglects the psychological factor in the use or contemplation of a 'practical' object. It is just that Munari prefers to solve the problem of decoration — so beset by rejection and glorification, from Adolf Loos up to the present day — in a democratic manner: he provides a very simple, colourless structure that can be 'completed' or 'decorated' by the user, in accordance with his own tastes and his own inclinations to follow one fashion or another. It is an 'unfinished' design which follows the precept of Lao Tzu: 'Production without appropriation
Action without imposition of self
Development without oppression.'

Let us take, for example, one of his productions from 1971: *Abitacolo* ('Cockpit' or 'Dwelling-place'). It is a structure made of plasticised steel which provides the bare minimum of living space and is intended to solve the problem of giving children their own space inside a normal family dwelling. *Abitacolo* is made up of 20-centimetre modules, with relevant sub-modules; it is a neutral shade of grey, without a trace of decoration; it is a compendium of pieces of furniture, since it combines a bed, a desk, a table, various containers, open surfaces and four ladders.

In his design work, Munari has always paid a great deal of attention to materials (each object had to be made out of the right material without any preconceived ideas about fashion or style) and to maximum simplicity of construction and use. In time, even his attitude towards the user has taken on an original complexion. In fact, Munari deliberately leaves his creations 'incomplete', refusing to colour them or add decoration, elements which he considers transient and to be determined by the personality and taste of the user.

Abitacolo, living structure for children, 1971.

Abitacolo, 1971.

In his presentation Munari writes:
'A light and trasparent den
or enclosure
a concealed space in the midst of people
a personal space
its presence makes furniture superfluous
the dust does not know where to settle
it is the minimum and it gives the maximum...'[7]

The last line cannot help but remind one of Mies van der Rohe's precept: 'less is more'. But Munari lowers the threshold of 'less' still further. *Abitacolo*, in fact, leaves total freedom to its owner, both in its uses and in its decoration. No dust settles on *Abitacolo*, not even the dust of continually changing fashion, while the limpid structure remains, without even imposing its own shadow. Munari is classical in his approach, since he looks for the rule, for formal coherence. But he rejects style, even his own, in design. For style signifies imposition of self, it means the addition of something that is not essential. This is why Munari organised an exhibition of objects produced by unknown designers: for anonymity guarantees objective inquiry.

But for Munari, 'anonymous' design must not interrupt the dialogue with the public. It is almost as if the pleasure he takes in designing is equal to the pleasure of making others understand his design. Hence he is always looking for the obvious, for what everyone always has before their eyes but no-one sees, through distraction, lack of education or habit. It seems that only he was able to discover that 'the square constructed on one side of a square is equal to the square constructed on any other side'.[8] Only Munari could see that there are *Roses in the salad*, or that one can produce beautiful patterns by cutting vegetables in half, pressing them on a pad of coloured ink and using them as a stamp. Munari is always offering facts and explanations to his public, often suggesting how his experiments may be repeated by supplying 'instructions for their use': in an age in which the possession of information is power, Munari 'squanders' it, an attitude consistent with his ethical code. Munari, in any case, is capable of being ironical about his activity as a designer, as well as about some of his theoretical assumptions, such as 'industrial naturalness'. In a text written in 1963, *Good design*, he does an ironical take-off of himself and his way of writing, by examining three natural 'objects' — the rose, the orange and peas — from the viewpoint of a designer. Thus peas were 'alimentary pills of various diameters, packed in bivalve containers that are extremely elegant in shape, material, odour, semi-transparency and remarkable ease of opening'. The orange on the other hand is 'an object made up of a series of modular containers in the shape of segments, arranged in a circle around a central vertical axis, on which each segment rests its straight side, while all the curved sides, facing outwards, produce together, as overall shape, a sort of sphere'.[9]

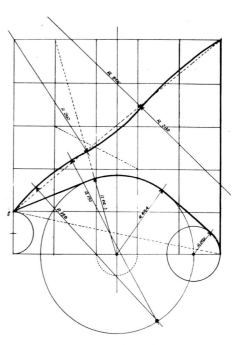

Design of a rose thorn, Indian ink on paper, 1963.

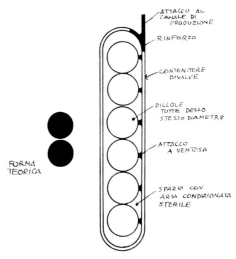

Design for peas if industrially manufactured, Indian ink, 1963.

'When the artist observes nature... it is as if nature communicated, through the sensitivity of the artist at the moment, one of its secrets,' Munari has written. This fidelity to nature, so similar to Leonardo's thought or Klee's sensibility, was applied to industrial design as well. This is evidenced both in his paradoxical observations of natural 'objects' studied as if they were industrial products, and in the method he followed for the actual manufacture of objects. The idea of 'industrial naturalness', or 'parallel nature', shows how Munari the designer was constantly on the look out for 'spontaneous' industrial forms and structures, as simple as possible and produced on the basis of principles of internal logic and formal coherence, rather than of style or tendency.

Indecipherable script of an unknown people, 1978.

Message in bottle with post scriptum, 1960.

Even when he was fighting his battle for 'good design' Munari knew how to enliven it with irony. As Giulio Carlo Argan has written, 'what saves him from methodologies and archetypologies of design is the way his objects and subjects mock themselves. Without this reciprocal irony, object and subject would be immovable and immutable.'[10]

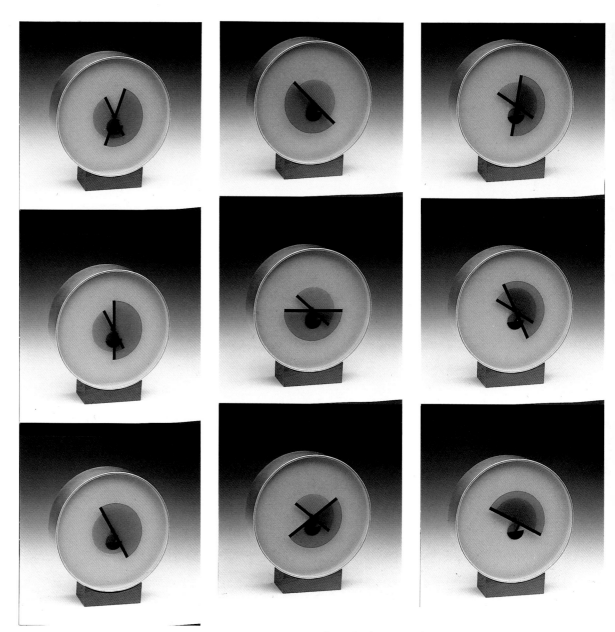

X hour, the first motor-driven
multiple, 1963.

His experiment with multiples, conducted in the early
1960s, was a generous attempt to give everyone the
possibility of enriching his own visual culture. Objects
in two or more dimensions — the most famous of
which was perhaps the *Flexy* — were made in large
numbers at low cost, using the methods of industrial
design, in order to communicate aesthetic information
to a broad and undifferentiated public.
But, like 'good design', the concept of the multiple
soon turned out to be a failure, revealing itself to be an
illusion incompatible with the demands of the market.

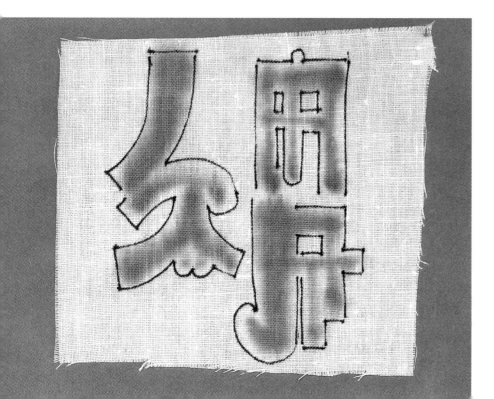

*Indecipherable script of an
unknown people*, 1960.

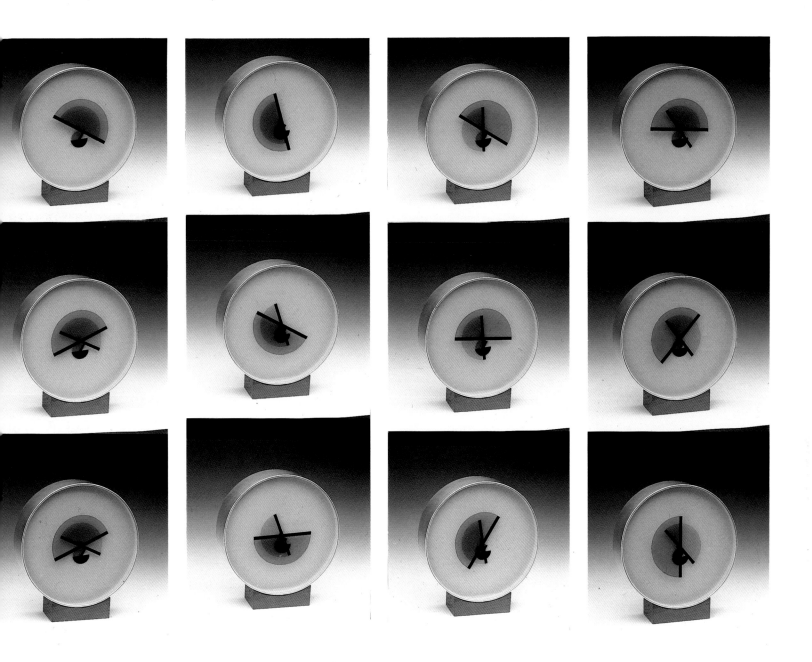

In the years following the war Munari carried on with the process of making the figure of the artist democratic, in part through a sort of cultural and technical bringing up to date. This meant new techniques of visual communication — like polarised light — and paying attention to 'Gestalt' research and theories, based on scientific suppositions. This was no mere modernisation of style, or infatuation with technology. Munari was simply convinced that 'the technological possibilities of our time make it possible for anyone to produce something that has aesthetic value'.[11] And a creative individual is a freer individual, because — asserts Munari — aesthetics vanquishes poverty and creativity helps one to adapt to reality. The artist and his relations with the public: this is a central theme in Munari's writings. He avoids populist overtones, but pursues the avowed aim of working so that the majority of free men may liberate their own creativity; a creativity with its own laws that have to be observed since, as Munari warns by quoting Valéry, the greatest freedom is only born out of the greatest stringency.

As is well known, Italy went through a period of strong economic growth at the beginning of the 1960s, placing it among the most heavily industrialised nations in the world. Italian design made its mark throughout the world and in 1962 one of the most enlightened Italian companies, Olivetti, sponsored the first exhibition of programmed art, presented by Umberto Eco. During the period Munari, along with Enzo Mari, the Gruppo T of Milan and the Gruppo N of Padua, appeared to hope that conditions could be created for projecting the image of an artist (or visual operator) able to bridge the gap between visual research and the public. But, as happened with 'good design', programmed art could not sustain such an illusion for long. Even an experiment like that of the 'multiples' was doomed to failure. The 'multiples' were objects designed by the same method as a research project is designed: the designer carries out an experiment on an optical or physical phenomenon, defines the elements of clarity of commination and makes a prototype. The prototype is not a one-off piece but a model for mass-production. Unlike art reproductions, which are no more than counterfeits of an original, the mass-produced pieces will always be superior to the prototype.

In contrast to the one-off piece, and to the arrogance of the Grand Opus, the multiple 'emerges already stripped of mystification in a large number of specimens'. They are industrially manufactured, at low cost, and help to broaden aesthetic awareness among a wider section of the public. 'Their aim is to propagate even simple notions of optics, chromatic perception, phenomena of accumulation, incredible problems of topology... in fact, by manipulating a multiple, the public is made directly aware of a phenomenon which will stay in its memory and make it see the world in which it lives in a different way.'[12]

So Munari was genuinely concerned with education. He carried on with this activity throughout the 1960s, publishing a variety of texts, some of which were polemic, others works of popularisation or strictly educational in their approach (although all three aspects can be found in each book): *Good design*, *Arte come mestiere* (Art as trade), *Artista e designer* (Artist and designer), *Fantasia* (Fantasy), *Design e comunicazione visiva* (Design and visual communication) and the recent *Da cosa nasce cosa* (From what comes what). Munari has illustrated or designed around sixty books, some forty of which he wrote himself: an amazing output. His approach to education has been distinctly anti-authoritarian, coming into conflict with the laws of the market-place and the cultural conditioning of adults. As a result, by the end of the 1960s, he had decided to concentrate largely on children, since they are 'less conditioned'. At a distance of twenty years the multiples produced by Munari are still fascinating. They are objects that invite you to reflect on the nature of colour and of light, on space and on topology, but there is always a contemplative side to them as well: Munari's man, Umberto Eco has remarked, is the restless inhabitant of an expanding universe, and needs to have a thousand eyes.

We have already mentioned *X hour*, conceived in 1945 but only put into mass production in 1963. We have looked at the *Continuous structures*. In 1965 came the *Tetracone*, a cube containing four cones, divided into two pairs in two complementary colours (red and green); the coloured cones — rotating around themselves by means of an electric motor — generate optical vibrations. A work of programmed art establishes a message to be put across and selects the proper means of expression without aesthetic or stylistic conditions, basing itself on physical, optical or scientific principles. Once again the aim is to eliminate subjective factors in order to communicate objective aesthetic information, common to all.

The last of Munari's multiples was produced in 1968: it was known as *Flexy*. When photographed it looks like one of Klee's sketches, but in reality it is a flexible module, a tetrahedron marked out in space by six steel wires. By manipulation it can be reduced to two dimensions, or a large series of patterns can be produced in space. Playing

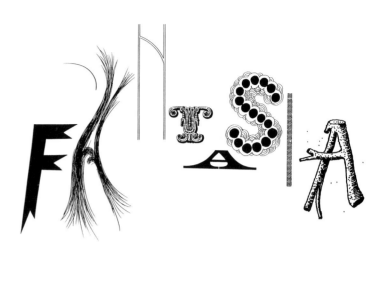

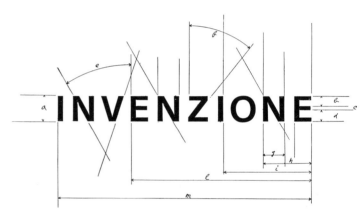

Flexy, multiple made out of metal wires, 1968.

CREATIVITA'

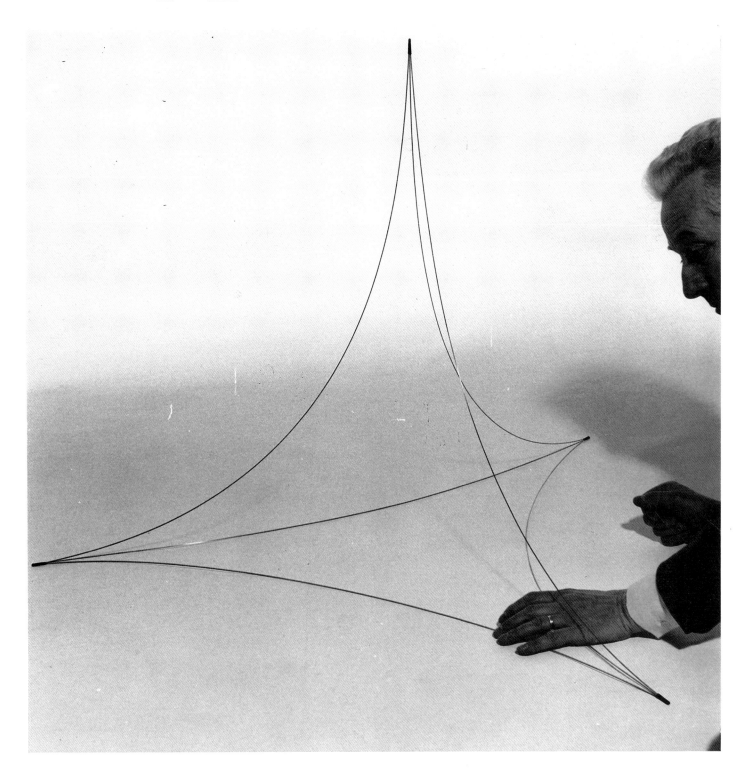

Children playing with a gigantic *Flexy*.

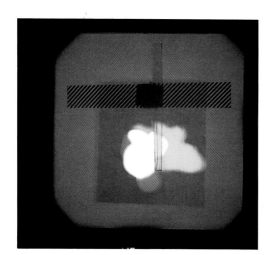

Projections with multifocal slides, 1953.

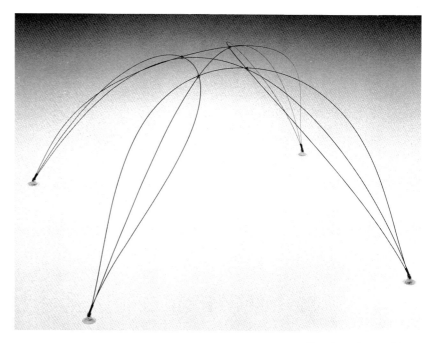

Flexy in various positions.

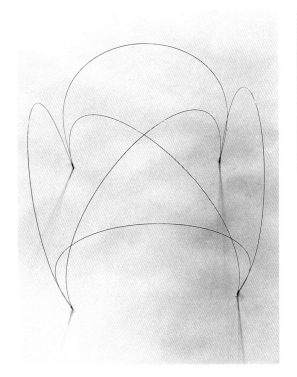

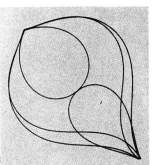

with it leads to an awareness of the aesthetic qualities present in a topological form. Munari's imagination was still running along the lines that had led him to create the *Travelling sculptures* in 1958. Small sculptures produced by making a few cuts and folds in a piece of card, the *Travelling sculptures* were akin to Balla's games or Albers's exercises at the Bauhaus: created out of two dimensions, they also owe something to Japanese origami. Small but tangible sculptures, they thumb their nose at unwieldy and irremovable works of sculpture. Their avowed purpose was the personalisation of communal spaces such as hotel rooms.

In the 1950s Munari began to achieve recognition for his efforts: he won the 'Compasso d'Oro' — the prize awarded annually by the association of Italian designers — in 1953 for a toy, little monkeys made of reinforced foam-rubber that could be placed in any desired position. He had an exhibition at the Museum of Modern Art in New York, where a number of his objects and posters are on permanent display. His name has won a renown that has increased over the years, resulting in him being invited to teach at a number of schools, and he is today an Honorary Member of the Carpenter Center of Visual Art Association at Harvard University. He has also held courses in Japan where he received an award in recognition of the high human quality of his design. Munari's influence, which has been at work in European culture for sixty years, has been, and still is, 'horizontal', in that it has been greater on a scholastic, educational level than in the field of art. And yet Munari has often anticipated movements and tendencies: his *Arhythmics* preceded Tinguely, his flattened trumpet César, his theories on unproductive machines predated Italian Situationism, while some of his manifestos, like the one he wrote in 1938, anticipated the advent of land art. In the meantime the critics were altering their view of his work. Previously they had only been aware of his playful side, or misunderstood him thoroughly, some even going so far as to claim he was an imitator of Calder. Munari has been written about by Eco, Argan, Ballo, Ragghianti (who dragged in Goethe on his behalf, giving the definition of 'accurate fantasy' to Munari's work), Fossati, Dorfles, Menna and many others in Italy; by Seuphor in France, Tachiguchi in Japan, Caroline Tisdall in England, etc.

Zizì baby monkey, second toy made out of reinforced foam-rubber, winner of the Compasso d'Oro, 1953.

The cat Meo, 1952.

Travelling sculptures, folded card, 1958.

Design for bas-relief, pencil on paper, 1948.

Prismatic folding lampshade, Danese, 1960.

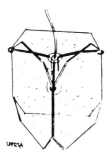

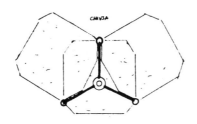

Travelling sculpture, brass, 1958.

Large folding sculpture, wood and man-made fibre, 1958.

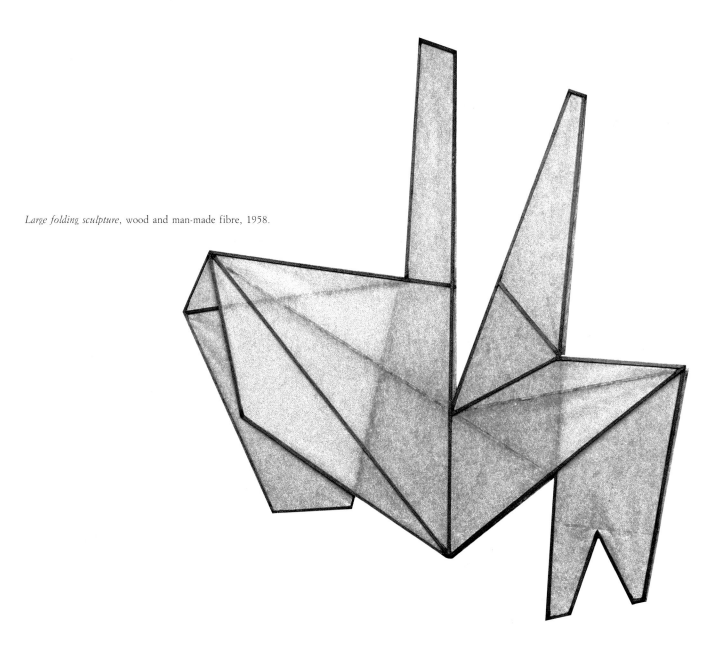

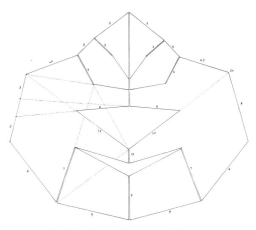

Design for *Travelling sculpture*, pencil on paper, 1958.

At the root of the *Travelling sculptures* lie perhaps the 'wooden flowers' of Balla, the didactic experiments of Albers, or Japanese origami. Apart from the paradoxical assumption (that these small sculptures made of card or wood and synthetic fibre can accompany us on our travels), they belong to the genre of European concrete art, the real source of these 'in-*stabiles*'. They can easily be folded up into two dimensions, thereby flying in the face of another academic convention.

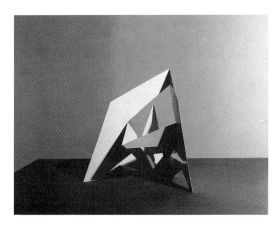

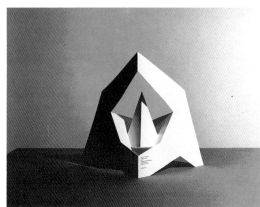

Different aspects of a single *Travelling sculpture*, folded card, 1958.

Travelling sculptures made out of different materials, 1958.

Even the patrons, both public and private, began to take notice of him, allowing him to tackle works on a considerable scale. Of these, Munari has always shown a preference for designing fountains. Naturally there is his relationship with water, which dates back to his childhood; and there is also the possibility of creating kinetic objects that exploit artificial and natural energies. The fountain he made for the Venice Biennale was based exclusively on sloping planes, moved by the water itself. His fountain for the Milan Trade Fair in 1961, on the other hand, was composed of two mobile, circular elements contained within another circular element: in this case each element was driven by a different force: water, air and electricity. In Tokyo, in 1964, he designed and installed a 'five-drop' fountain. This simple device allowed exactly five drops of water to fall at regular intervals, each one at a pre-arranged point, thereby creating concentric and proportionate ripples that intersected one another. There are very few contemporary artists with the ability to exploit so suggestively the union between nature and technology, seeking an inner naturalness in the latter. It has led him to realisations that enter an area of research which induced Klee to write: 'We should want something similar — a basic similarity — to what is created by nature: not something that sets out to compete with her, but something that signifies: here is how it is in nature'.[13]

Fountain of inclined planes, Venice Biennale, 1954.

Illustration for *Nella nebbia di Milano*, 1968.

83

Montecatini fountain, Fiera di Milano, 1952.

Directly connected with Munari's store of childhood imagery are his fountains, for the most part created for exhibitions or fairs and therefore short-lived. A natural source of energy is almost always used to move the elements of these fountains: water, air and wind. Outstanding among them for its poetic simplicity is the one he constructed in Tokyo in 1965, where a mere five drops of water, falling at pre-arranged points, created a fascinating pattern of concentric ripples.

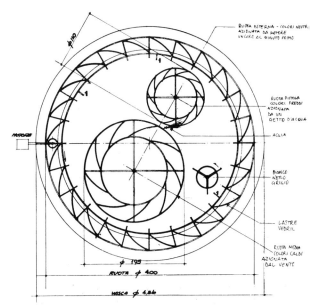

Blades of a water-mill.

Whirlpool in the river.

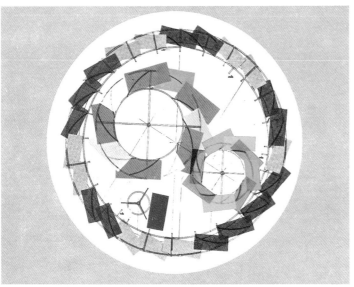

Designs for the *Montecatini fountain*, made out of sheets of transparent plastic. The wheels were turned by a motor and the action of wind and air.

Water-mill on the Adige.

Munari in his studio. Above, the first *Concave convex*, behind him a *Useless machine* from 1933 and, in his hands, a sculpture made out of brass wire, 1949.

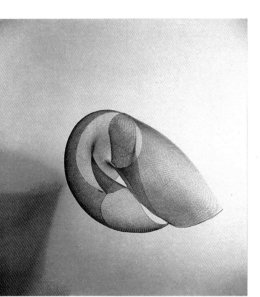
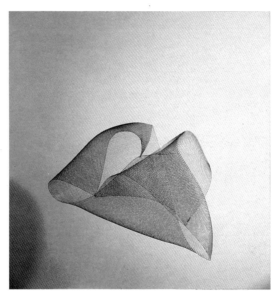
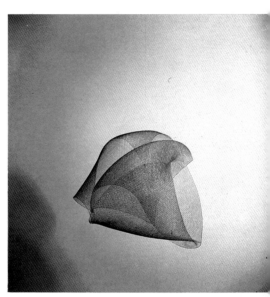

Different views of the same *Concave convex*, 1947.

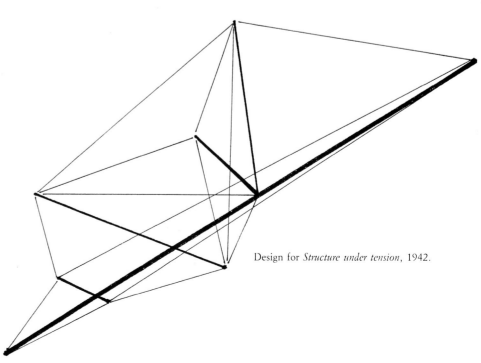

Design for *Structure under tension*, 1942.

Concave convex, object made out of bent wire mesh, 1947.

Nor has there been any break in Munari's graphic activity
since the first world war. Along with some other great
names in international graphic art, such as Albe Steiner
and Max Huber, Munari was invited to reorganise the style
of graphics used by the publishing house Einaudi, but he
has also worked for a number of other prestigious
publishers, such as Mondadori, Bompiani and Editori
Riuniti.

In Munari's approach to graphics, one finds no concession
to the superfluous: his covers introduce the subject with
pertinent, but never purely illustrative images. At other
times, as in the case of the cover he designed for Editori
Riuniti, one finds a severe perceptual statement,
reminiscent of constructivism.

In the last few years, he has avoided the traditional break
between text, illustrations, notes and captions in the layout
of his books, making them up without jumps or
interruptions. He merely uses different sizes of type,
allowing the book to be read in a way that is not rigidly
predetermined, but free, 'as if the book were a single
continuous sheet, as wide as a page but as long as all the
pages set one below the other'. Moreover, as early as 1949
he had brought out his *Unreadable books*, a group of books
so called because they contained no text, just an exclusively
visual story, recounted with geometric figures, transparent
sheets, or sheets of tracing paper, with pages that were
perforated or torn or pierced by a thread, rigid sheets and
black or coloured ones. Thus the story was told through
the possibilities provided by typography, paper-making and
binding, through the structural components of the book as
an autonomous, concrete object, no longer a mere container
for literary ideas.

However, Munari has also designed and realised books in
which the literary account goes hand in hand with the
visual one. This is the case, for example, with the
extraordinary *Nella nebbia di Milano* (In the Milan fog),
where sheets of tracing paper produce a poetically misty
effect; through them one makes out, faintly at first and
then more and more distinctly, the shapes of trees and the
lights of the city.

Even in his books there is no compulsory route, and it is
the reader's hand that is allowed continuously to shift the
point of view, in the spirit of these works: there is a
predisposition to change in response to changes in the
recipient, who is invited to 'touch with his own hand' in
order to check the functioning of the work and of his own
perceptual system.

Covers for *Unreadable books*, 1951.

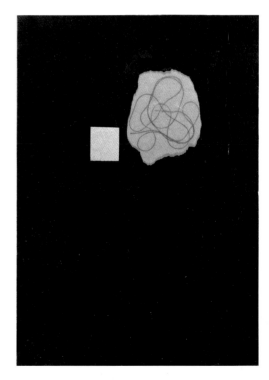

Unreadable book, published by Mastrella, 1983.

Unreadable book, published by Corraini, 1984.

As long ago as the 1930s Munari had been trying out radical innovations in graphics and typography, such as the insertion of a transparent sheet between two opaque pages. But it was not until after the war (apart from the case of the interesting but unpublished *Dada almanac* of 1940) that he began to design and produce book-objects, made up without a text but exploiting all the technical possibilities of printing and paper-making, in order to tell a visual story, released from subjection to the literary text.

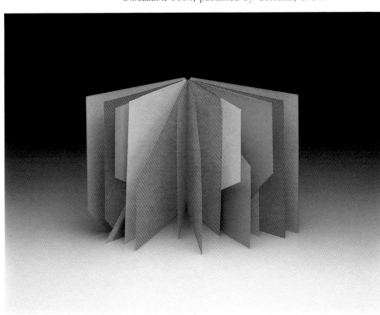

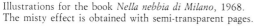

Illustrations for the book *Nella nebbia di Milano*, 1968.
The misty effect is obtained with semi-transparent pages.

Bruno Munari presents a number of
objects where a reconciliation is achieved
between fantasy and a technique that
had led him on other occasions to the
creation of the *Useless machines*. The
harsh or soft colours that he arranges in
two or three dimensions, the multiple
values that result from this, appear,
when first perceived, arbitrary or even to
function as symbols. However, these
objects stem from a constructive
necessity of a popular nature, one that
demands the miracle of several bodies
packed into a limited space, the same
notion that in another age saw precious
sailing ships squeezed into bottles.
                    Salvatore Quasimodo, 1940

Bonsai of an oleander bush grown by Munari.

Metaphysical object, various materials under bell jar, 1946.

91

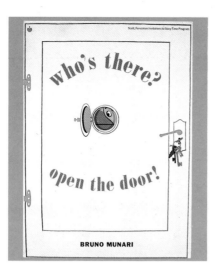

Illustrations from his first book for children, 1945.

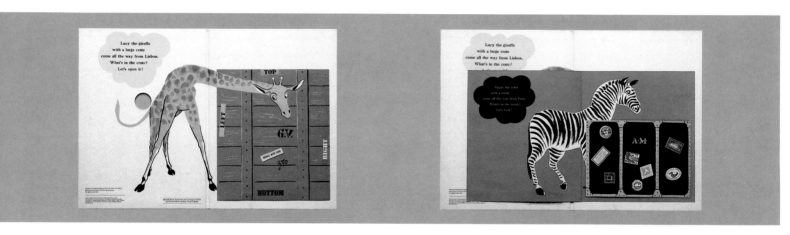

Illustration from the book *Mai contenti*, 1945.

Munari playing with children.

Towards an art for everyone

Cubic lampshade, manufactured by Danese, 1958.

Munari is a man small in stature, well-proportioned, rapid in his movements, always ready for a friendly argument and for a demonstration — theoretical or practical — of his ideas. He is a person of rare courtesy, who never refuses an interview to anyone. His accessibility and urbanity have been stressed by critics, journalists and by the ordinary people with whom he comes in contact. Between Munari the man and Munari the artist there are no discrepancies. Faithful to his own anti-romantic principles, he has led a tranquil outer existence, interrupted by the occasional working trip. He has never been troubled by inner doubts or artistic crises, and only rarely has his irony taken a bitter turn: when he recalls how many critics saw him as nothing more than a curiosity for twenty or thirty years; when he admits that his attempt to broaden the public for art — an attempt made by means of programmed art and his multiples — has failed, owing in part to the implacable nature of the laws of the market-place, in part to the lack of cultural preparation on the part of consumers; when he remarks that often even little children have already been conditioned by a 'Disney' culture.

He has always taken the trouble to present his own work, to explain its underlying causes and intentions, to the point where it becomes performance art.

As far back as the 1950s he pointed out that many articles of design had existed long before the term 'design' became part of contemporary culture. Hence he has proposed presenting an award to all those obscure designers, most of them unknown; who were responsible for objects still in common use today; objects like the deck-chair, folding chairs, the garage lamp, window-dressers' equipment and so on, 'appropriate and well-made articles,' explains Munari, 'that have been in production for many years because they are well made and not because they bear someone's signature.'[1]

There is no hiding his disdain for styling, that sort of cosmetic design which Munari, along with all the designers linked to the current of 'good design', has been combatting for years, precisely because it is not essential. Strongly influenced by fashion, cosmetic design is something 'extra' that often obscures the purpose of the object and complicates it unnecessarily. In fact Munari accepts the distinction made by Moles, according to whom an object whose elements belong to many different classes is complicated, whereas the object with a large number of elements that belong to only a few classes is complex. An article of 'good design' can be complex, but not complicated.

Preparatory designs for the *Cubic lampshade*.

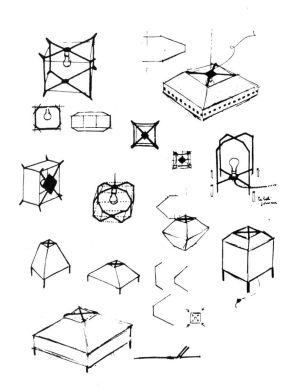

Bamboo vase and designs for bamboo vases for
a Japanese craftsman, 1965.

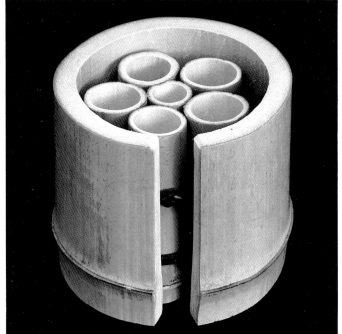

Several bamboo vases.

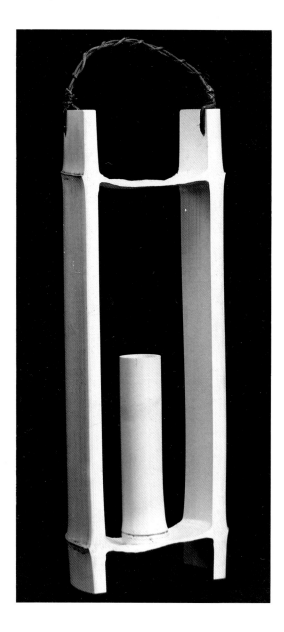

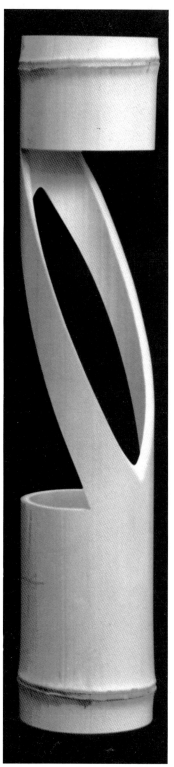

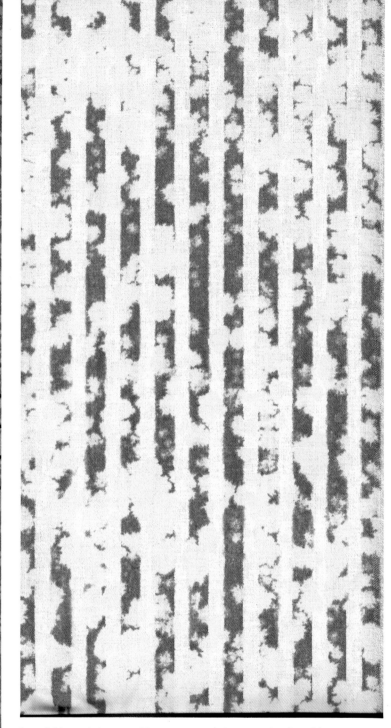

Printed fabrics, Assia, 1983. No preparatory designs exist for these fabrics, since Munari applied printing techniques directly onto the fabric.

His proposal to award a prize to anonymous designers is at once ironic and polemical. Just as the artist has to invade life with his art, the designer should not confine himself to designing lamps, ashtrays and cutlery but work on the whole human environment. This is why he has recently suggested designing anew the avenues of the city — in conformity with his artistic origins and with that manifesto of 1934 in which he proposed artistic intervention in the environment itself, anticipating the artistic tendency now known as land art. According to Munari, a row of trees that are all the same is the ideal of a filing clerk, not of a gardener. Why not avoid banality and repetition when planting trees and flower beds? One could arrange a variety of compositions, using different plants that come into flower at different seasons, whether they are evergreen or deciduous: 'in an avenue of this kind people would take more pleasure in walking, and find each other more easily: come and visit me, I live at the third magnolia, I can smell the perfume of its flowers from my window'.[2] And he finishes up his remarks with a rigorous analysis of all the problems connected with the proposal. Munari's 'exact fantasy' is aimed here at making the poetry and the beauty which could improve our lives tangible, but he does it with precision, leaving no room for pipe dreams.

Munari — like many other Western artists — is fascinated by Oriental culture and finds many elements in it that are consonant with his own ideas: 'One thing that I learned in Japan is just this aspect of design that has to take into account the senses of the user, all his senses, for when he is confronted with an object he probes it, he feels it with all his senses'.[3] Munari, the great eclectic, could not fail to appreciate a culture that teaches you to stay within nature, rather than to dominate it. A mark of this attitude was a performance that he put on in Como in 1969, to which he gave the title *Showing the air*. Together with the audience he dropped a number of 'shapes revealing the air' from the top of a tower. These consisted of various sheets of paper folded or cut in such a way that they behaved differently as they fell, describing virtual volumes determined by the movement of the air currents. It was an event with Futurist precedents (Corra and Settimelli, 1914) but it is also reminiscent of Duchamp, who obtained his unit of measure by dropping a ruler from a height. However, it also and above all demonstrates that coincidence with Zen culture which the Japanese have recognised in Munari on more than one occasion. It suffices to quote — in analogy with *Showing the air* — this line from an ancient Zen poem: 'The trees show the bodily form of the wind'.

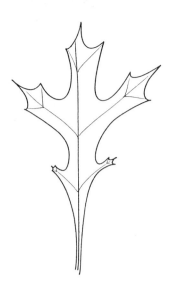

Pencil on paper, 1981.

Munari's interest in children is probably partly the result of the disappointment he received in the mid 1960s, with the failure of his concept of 'good design' and when his experiments with programmed art and the multiple did not receive the support from the public that he had so optimistically hoped for.
If the mentality of adults was already so ossified, thought Munari, then it was to children, still capable of liberating or retaining their own creativity, that he had to turn.

Working with children at the Museum of Modern Art in Ciudad Bolivar, Venezuela, 1984.

In connection with the studies of Piaget, Munari has created, alone or in collaboration with educational experts, games or toys that set out to convey the maximum amount of information to children, making use of the entire sensory apparatus, in order to help them form a creative and elastic mentality. As in his more recent works of design, his toys are often 'incomplete', awaiting the participation of the children themselves. This also goes to show that by now Munari is pursuing through a wide range of activities a single strategy of intervention in the world of children as well as in that of adults.

Working with children at a school in Milan, 1970.

Working with children at the Kodomo no Shiro in Tokyo, 1985.

Working with children at the Museum of Modern Art in Ciudad Bolivar, Venezuela, 1984.

Zen also represents a point of contact between some features of the teachings of Munari and of Klee. One Zen quotation that Munari returns to again and again is that 'change is the only constant in the universe'. And for both Munari and Klee, the important thing is not to arrive at the finished and forever fixed form; what matters is the ability to alter experience, the readiness to produce all over again, the 'work that becomes'. Eternal motion invalidates the idea of a final result: 'the way to form', wrote Klee, 'transcends its destination, goes beyond the end of the way itself'.[4]

When he was devising rules governing the techniques of communication with children, Munari concluded as follows: 'Sixth: destroy everything and do over', since 'destruction of the collective work, in this particular case and period of infancy, should be seen as a way to avoid the creation of models for imitation, the refusal to put the work in a museum, the rejection of star status for its author'.[5] Destroying everything means 'transcending the goal', going beyond the idea of a final outcome. This is why we have also spoken of Munari's irony as temporality, the fourth dimension: since, by destroying all that he had said and done in the past, he rouses the creative spirit to action again.

From *Alfabetiere*,
Einaudi, 1960.

Leonardo's diagram on
the growth of plants.

Roses in the salad, prints made
from sectioned vegetables, 1983.

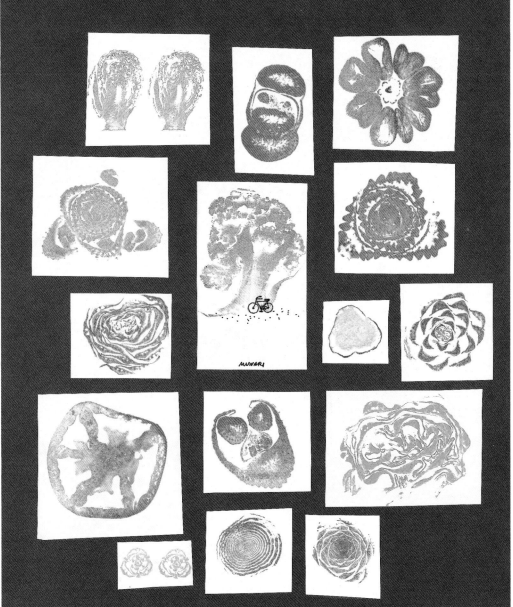

101

So the two artists suggested that their students should avoid preconceived ideas and the rigid imitation of models; however it is important to practise the imitation of systems of construction and not the finished form, in order to learn to recognise 'what is flowing underneath, the prehistory of the visible'.[6] Hence there are different aspects to reality, which we are often incapable of seeing. Therefore rigid metal schemes should not be allowed to get in the way of the stimulus that leads to creation; Munari suggested to his pupils that they should not think before they act, not let any ideas come before tackling a composition. A remark by the Zen philosopher Shen Hui is highly appropriate: 'If working with the mind is equivalent to disciplining one's own mind, how can this be called liberation?'. It is a way that sets up a dynamic equilibrium between rational and irrational (as we have already seen in many of Munari's works), an attempt to remain within the flow of life even while carrying out an artistic operation. In the hidden structures of nature, Munari and Klee are seeking the relationship between the artistic product, the artificial one and nature. For Klee the purpose of this investigation is to 'capture the image in the pure state', by looking for its

archetype; for Munari it is the discovery of the ultimate structure of organic things, and its laws, in order to reveal its formal coherence and transpose it into the world of art and design.

For both, in any case, 'the dialogue with nature remains the *conditio sine qua non*; the artist is man, he himself is nature, fragment of nature in the domain of nature',[7] as Klee has written. It is up to art to impose order on eternal movement, through a process that leads from quantity to quality, from chaos to order. An 'allegory of creation' Klee calls it; a 'parallel nature' notes Munari — by way of participation in nature, not opposition to it. The two artists also concur in pointing out that one may teach technique, the laws of creation and their exceptions, but not originality or art.

These, in brief, are the points where Klee and Munari coincide in their teaching, an accord that one finds more rarely in their work: a certain preference for the linear style, for a predominance of graphic elements, an incisive mark here or there, or a few objects of investigation, like the leaf, dating back to 1942-43.

Their views diverge where Klee contrasts the prosaic nature of life with the poetry of art: 'learn to appreciate seeing yourself transposed into a world that, by entertaining you, gives you strength for the inevitable return to the dreariness of the everyday'.[8] Munari, on the other hand, maintains that there should be no split between art and

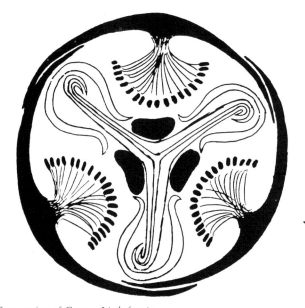

Cross-section of German Iris before its opening, Indian ink on paper, 1951.

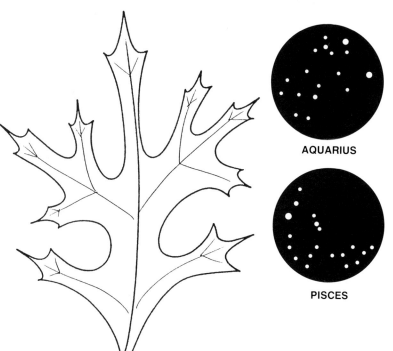

AQUARIUS

PISCES

 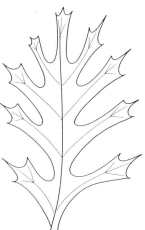   

Variations on an oak leaf, pencil on paper, 1951.

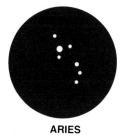

ARIES

VIRGO

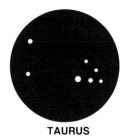

TAURUS

LIBRA

GEMINI

SCORPIO

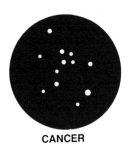

CANCER

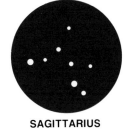

SAGITTARIUS

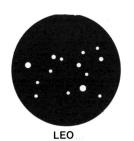

LEO

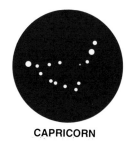

CAPRICORN

Constellations of the Zodiac, perforated silver discs. Held up against the light, the holes form different constellations. Manufactured by Ricci, 1975.

103

life, since there ought not to be 'a false world in which to live materially and an ideal world in which to take refuge morally'.[9] Munari would subscribe to Klee's ideas about the roving point of view and the danger of 'form as repose', as well as to phrases like 'irregularity signifies greater freedom without violation of the law'[10] or the observation that formalism is form without function. But Klee has had no direct influence on Munari's visual work, apart from in his biro sketches (the *Birobotanics* 1952) or the colour drawings *Presence of the ancestors* (1966), in which he lets himself go in an investigation of the face. An investigation that he returned to, in 1970, with *Let's look each other in the eye*, a series of sheets of paper on which faces are produced through drawing and/or tears; the sheets can be superimposed and the result is a continual change in the colour of the 'eyes'. The lesson: 'Only he who has a different visual opening can see the world in another way and can pass on to his neighbour the information required to broaden his field of view... let us get used to looking at the world through the eyes of others'.[11] And yet here it turns out that the joy and delight of drawing has got the upper hand of didactics.

Let's look each other in the eye, movable and superimposable pieces of card, 1970.

Munari's grandson alongside a bonsai cultivated by his grandfather.

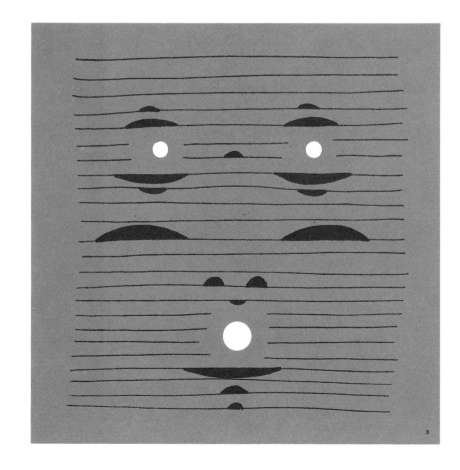

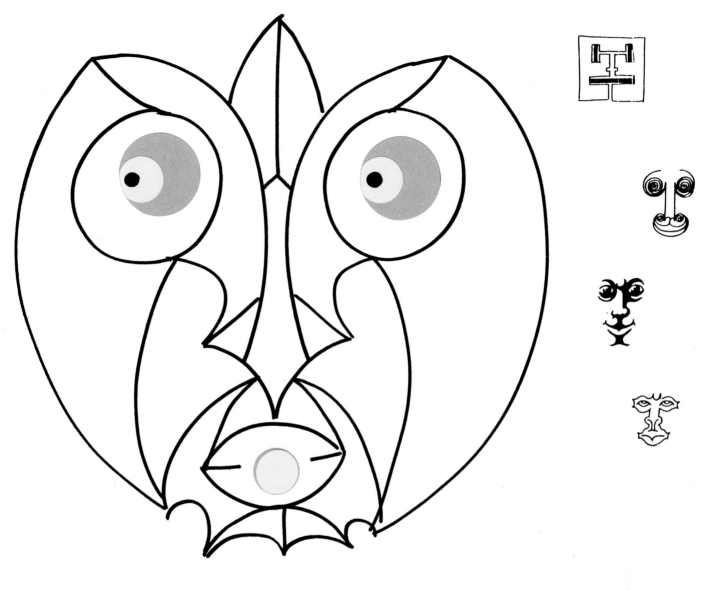

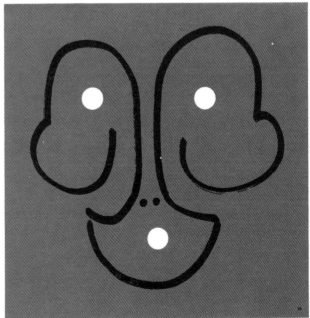

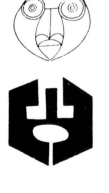

Variations of the human face, felt-tip pen on paper, 1951.

In 1965 Munari began to work out a simple technique for producing images, which is important in conceptual terms as well. But let us go back for a moment to the multiples. As we have seen, a large number of the multiples were produced, both in order to reach a wider public and to challenge the 'one-off piece'. Umberto Eco, who was a theoretical supporter of Munari during the phase of programmed art, observes in his *Trattato di semiotica generale* (Treatise on general semiotics) that 'duplicating is neither representing nor imitating... but reproducing, by the same processes, the same conditions'. So this is how it is with the multiples, that are produced directly in unlimited series, each perfectly identical to the other. The 'one-off piece', for instance a painting by Raphael, 'seems to be beyond any possibility of duplication... since he invented the rule of production while he was producing... thereby carrying out an action that set up a code'.[12]

In simple terms, the multiple can be duplicated without limit since the project (the rule of production) is separate from the execution, while the one-off piece is such because project and execution occur at the same instant.

Let us look now at the rule of production for the *Original xerographs*. The technique is a very simple one: using an ordinary photocopying machine new images are obtained by moving the original picture for the five seconds that it takes the light to move across the exposure screen. Munari has achieved remarkable results by making use of textures and moiré effects, but also with photographic images, such as the one of a motorcyclist (and remembering a naively Futurist sketch of his from 1927, *Dynamism of a motorcyclist*, makes one realise how much distance he has covered on those two wheels during the course of fifty years).

Munari has remarked that producing the *Original xerographs* is like drawing with surfaces instead of with lines. In this process can be found many of the themes which have absorbed Munari's interest over the many decades of his artistic career: the machine used for irregular, aesthetic ends; his passion for opposites: a machine that reproduces passively is turned into a machine that produces actively; the use of light and movement; the intervention of the user; the reference to the experiences of the historical avant-garde, in this case Man Ray and his research into photograms. But there is more.

The *Xerographs* obtained in this manner are called *original* because they are not reproducible, 'because to reproduce them the creative process would have to be repeated'. That is to say it would be necessary to reproduce the 'rule of production' invented during the production: which, if it is impossible for a painting by Raphael, is also impossible for these *Xerographs* since, as Munari explains, 'to make a photocopy of it would be to cancel all its most perceptible nuances'.[13]

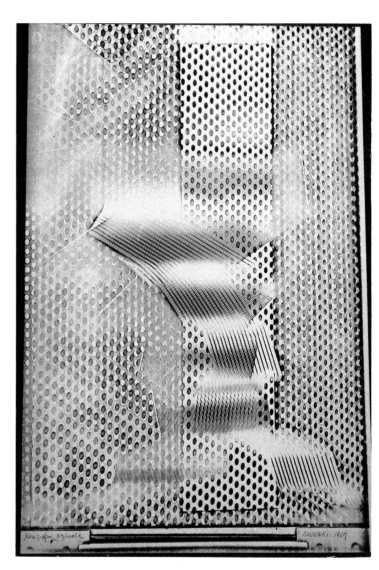

Original xerograph, 1969, Biondi collection.

Motorcyclist, pencil on paper, 1927.

Motorcyclist, original xerograph, 1968.

Original xerograph, 1978.

It is the exact opposite of the multiple: the *Original xerographs* refute reproducibility and duplication (even though they were produced on a machine that is normally used to make faithful reproductions); hence they unexpectedly reintroduce the 'one-off piece'.

But there is no contradiction here, in that these one-off pieces no longer have an 'aura' of their own. They are within the reach of all, testable and not the object of passive contemplation. Munari himself realised the 'artistic' limits of the *Xerographs*, but this time he was more concerned with their educational, demonstrative aspect. Even low-cost works of art, he writes, carry the spirit of genius with them, leaving the public with an inferiority complex. The task of the contemporary artist is to try out artistic instruments and then present them to the public at large. Today technology 'makes it possible for anyone who has got rid of his inferiority complex with regard to art, to bring into play his own creativity that has been humiliated for so long'.[14]

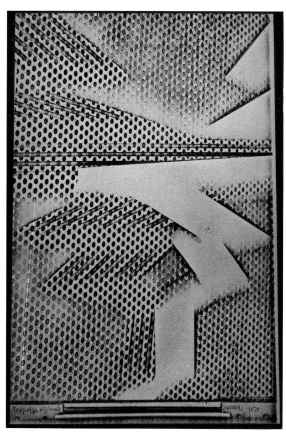

Original xerograph, 1965, Biondi collection.

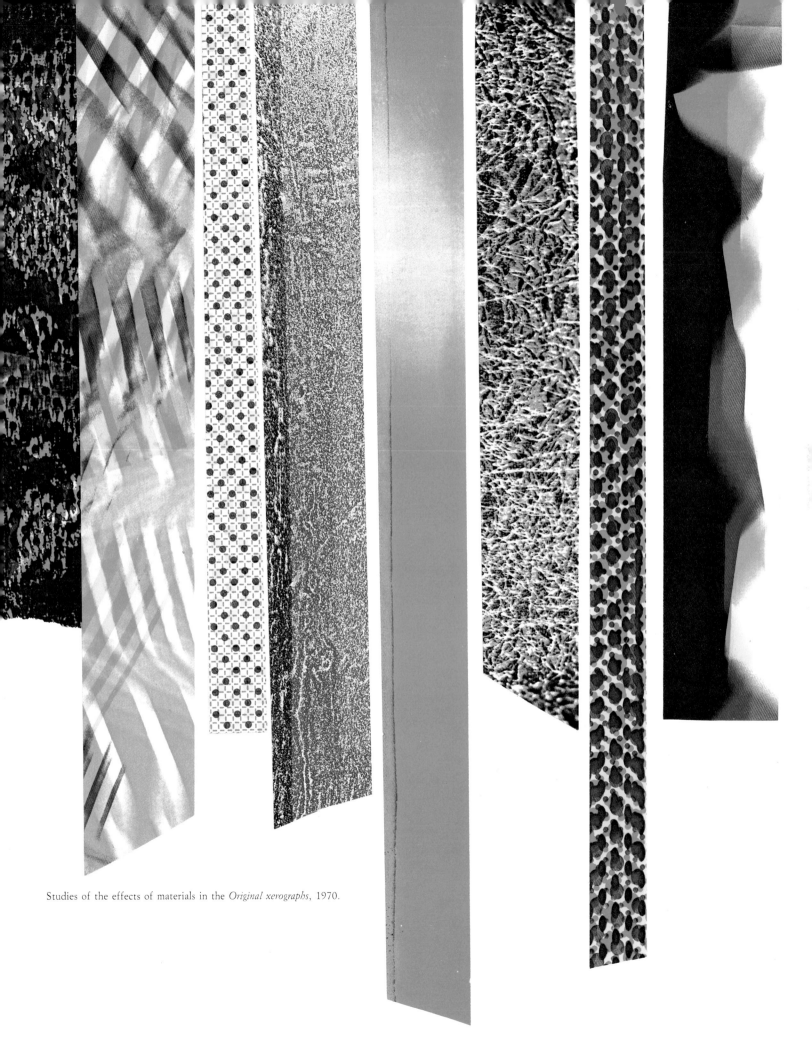

Studies of the effects of materials in the *Original xerographs*, 1970.

We have already mentioned the fact that over the last decade Munari has turned his attention largely towards children, towards the preservation and development of their creativity. But he was already interested in children as long ago as the 1940s, at a time when he was designing and producing numerous books for children. His incentive for doing so seemed accidental: his desire to provide his own son Alberto (who, ironically or by predestination, is today head of the Department of Psychology and Pedagogy at the University of Geneva) with more suitable books than were available at the time. Munari notes that the children of today do not know what princesses and knights are: 'when one talks to somebody, whether a child or an adult, it is necessary to begin with what he knows and then take him far away in the imagination'.[15] His stories are simple and delightfully but clearly illustrated. They were published, in part, by Mondadori and subsequently in the United States, where they were fairly successful. It is also worth recalling his illustrations for the books of Gianni Rodari, the famous writer of children's tales. For *La torta in cielo* he returned to his investigation of faces for the *Ancestors* series, rendering them by the use of lines and points; or by a simple accumulation of points he obtained the effect of a crowd viewed from above as it flowed into a square.

In *Favole al telefono*, the central character is a travelling salesman who tells fairy-stories to his child every evening over the telephone; for this book Munari produced illustrations which, explains the artist, 'resemble those drawings which you make while you are on the telephone, they have something to do with the content, but they are partly unconscious doodles.'[16] As well as children's books, Munari has designed a number of toys. We have already mentioned his flexible dolls made out of reinforced foam-rubber, for which he was awarded the 'Compasso d'Oro' in 1953. But his pedagogic research became increasingly important, and began to play a predominant role in his work.

The reasons for this interest are twofold: on the one hand his constant effort to improve on what he considers badly done, his determination not to repeat slavishly the experiences of others or ingrained habits; on the other, his desire to make a greater impression on the public, by getting to it before it is completely culturally conditioned: 'we must look after the children and give the children the chance to form a freer, more elastic and less blocked mentality, capable of making decisions. And I would say, a method for dealing with reality too, as a desire for both understanding and expression. So, to this end, study should be made of these instruments that take the form of playthings but which, in reality, help man to liberate himself.'[17] An ambitious and generous scheme, behind which one can detect Munari's disappointment with his lack of contact with the general public, a dialogue that he himself has pressed for but which was evidently utopian, or premature.

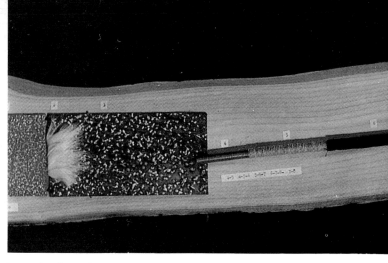

Tactile board, wood and other materials, 1943.

The didactic spirit with which Munari is imbued has led him to seek a distinction between fantasy and creativity, a distinction that is often at the root of his most important works. Fantasy, in fact, 'is a faculty of the mind that makes it possible to invent mental images that differ from reality in details or as a whole, images that may be impossible to realise in practical terms', while creativity 'is a productive capacity, where imagination and reason are combined, so that the result obtained can always be practically realised'.

Pre-books, 1979. Books designed for children who are not yet able to read. Made out of a variety of materials, they involve the whole of the child's sensory apparatus.

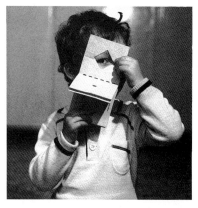

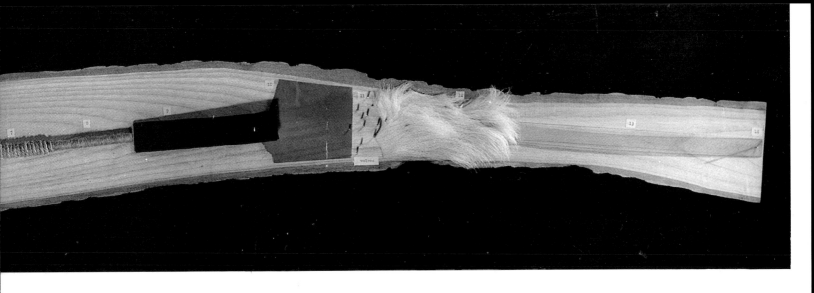

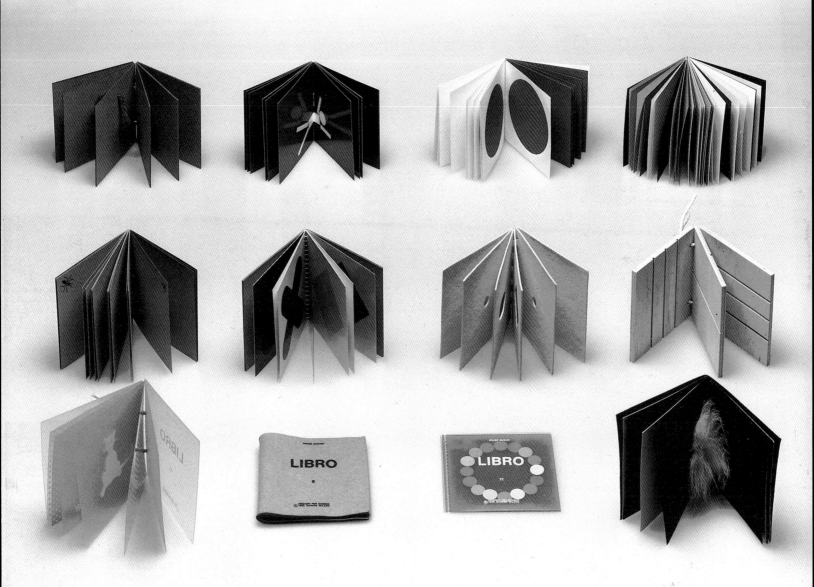

His toys, some of which were designed in collaboration with Nino Belgrano, include one from 1971 called *More and Less*, with which he returns to the theme of transparent sheets that can be superimposed, encouraging children to use their imagination to construct continually changing patterns. Munari has pointed out that toys are usually chosen by adults not on the basis of their educational value, but for other reasons. The toy, in Munari's view, should cater to all the child's senses — this is a constant feature of Munari's thinking as an artist and designer. Therefore it should not be disagreeable or banal and it must be possible for a small child to manipulate it — for he has to try it out — while a purely decorative toy is useless.

Like some of his more recent design work, Munari's toys and games are often 'unfinished', since they must be completed and modified by their user: once again they require active participation and not passive contemplation. Munari's pedagogy — undoubtedly influenced by the work of Piaget — is based on recognition of a simple fact: fantasy, imagination and creativity operate by establishing relations with what is in everyone's memory. Fantasy can come up with things that are unattainable in practice, unlike inventiveness which operates on the practical plane. Creativity brings about a fusion between fantasy and inventiveness, while the imagination — finally — serves to picture that which creativity, fantasy and inventiveness produce in the memory.

This is why a three-year-old child already needs the right kind of toys: for it is at this age that he memorises the sensory experiences provided by his surroundings. So a designer can produce a game or toy 'that communicates to the child, the adult in the making, the maximum of information that he can handle and that is, at the same time, an instrument for the formation of a flexible and non-repetitive mind'.[18] In this one seems to hear an echo of the words of Balla and Depero.

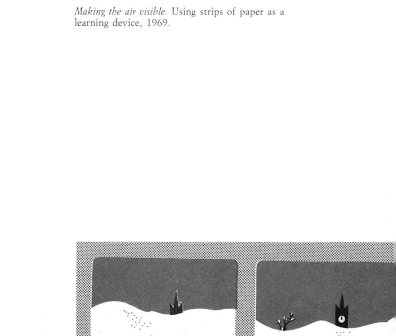

Making the air visible. Using strips of paper as a learning device, 1969.

Playing cards, educational game (with Nino Belgrano), produced by Danese, 1968.

first workshop for children at Brera, Milan.

To this end Munari has designed the *Pre-books*, one of his more recent productions (1980). These are twelve small books made out of many different materials: transparent plastic, cloth, paper, wood, etc. The child playing with the *Pre-books* receives a wide range of information through his senses: the *Pre-books* 'tell' simple stories, stories that are not written but visual, tactile, sonorous, thermal and physical.

'They ought to give the impression that books are objects made in such a way and that they contain a wide variety of surprises. Culture is made up of surprises... and it is necessary to be ready to take them in and not reject them for fear that the castle we have built for ourselves might collapse.'[19]

We must be as mutable as nature herself, Klee would say. Yet another step towards 'ludopedagogy' — i.e. education through play — has been taken by Munari with the setting up of workshops for children. The first came into operation in 1976, at the Brera museum in Milan, in collaboration with Franco Russoli. Again one might see a Futurist lack of reverence in this invasion of a place traditionally connected with seriousness and contemplation, by a myriad of children gathered together not to 'learn' passively, but to liberate their own creativity.

The workshops, labelled as 'playing with art', have the function of making children familiar with the language of visual communication, without restrictions and without assignments to be carried out. Through their play, the children become accustomed to visual observation, to classification, to relating different objects to each other and to trying unusual combinations. Like Munari the artist and designer, they grow accustomed to looking for what is hidden beneath the surface of things. A child who learns that the sky is not always and only blue, for example, is — in Munari's view — a child who will probably find more creative solutions to a problem in future; who will be more ready to argue and no to submit.

Workshops for children are functioning in various parts of the world today and Munari — who makes use of videotapes and of a host of collaborators (resembling a mediaeval *bottega*) — has extended his influence as far as Japan and South America. An influence that is — as we have already pointed out — 'horizontal', an influence that has been much stronger on the level of primary-school teaching than in the world of contemporary art.

Stones found, drawn on or rearranged by Munari.

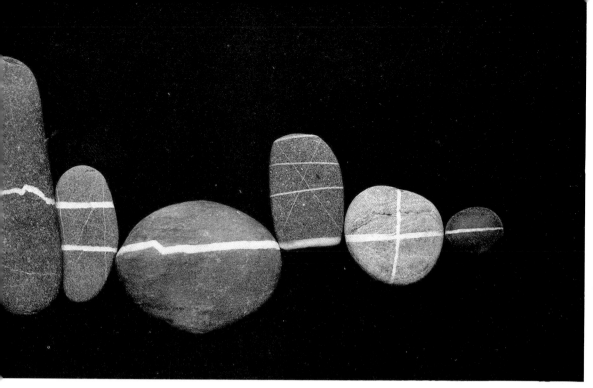

115

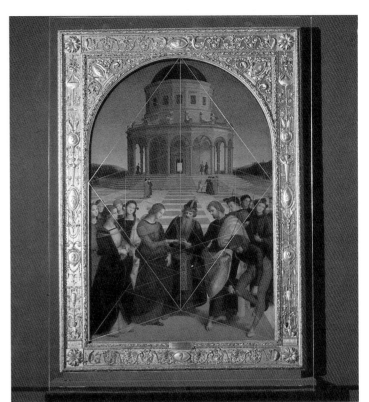

In 1977 numerous artists were invited to comment, through their own works, on the works of art on display in the Brera museum. Munari set up a transparent screen that allowed the public to perceive the probable harmonic structure of Raphael's *The betrothal of the Virgin Mary*.

Impassive stone, found at Riva Trigoso.

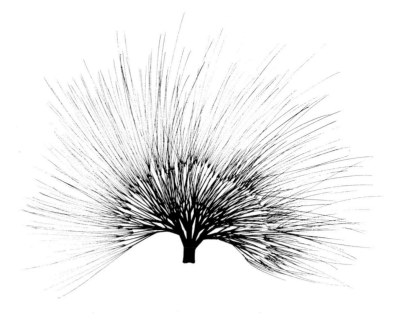

Research into a comprehensive habitable structure in four blocks: hygiene facilities, kitchen, living-room, bedroom. The structure is intended to be adaptable to any living space. Designed with the architects Lorenzo Davanzati and Piero Ranzani, 1968.

A world, however, that sees him as much more of a protagonist today, an artist who has traversed its territory far and wide and — it could be said on looking back — obliquely and transversely. His figure still remains an 'anomalous' one and yet we have seen that it has never been an isolated one: Futurist among Futurists, abstractionist among abstractionists, with close ties to the trends that have changed the face of contemporary graphics; a moving spirit in concrete art and in 'good design', a theoretician of programmed art. In Munari we find here and there echoes of the ideas and themes of Gropius, Moholy-Nagy and Albers, as of the Russian constructivists; of Man Ray, Duchamp and Arp, as well, of course, as Marinetti and Balla. He owes something to much of contemporary art, which owes much to him. He has been responsible for important ideas, often central to the interests of the best of European culture, concerned with the machine and technology, with nature and planning, with the useful and the gratuitous, with play, children and tomorrow's society — all accompanied by a pure sense of humour and a subtle and penetrating irony. His works testify to a superior balance of mind, and give an impression of calm complexity:

'art léger comme une musique... un air à variations à la fois riche e simple, à la manière de Mozart,[20] is how Michel Seuphor has described it.

'An open, mutable and natural art,' Shuzo Takiguchi has written, 'that looks almost miraculous today, but is not a miracle, just the true human shape of Bruno Munari.'[21] And, finally, his contribution to the liberation of children's creativity. 'Culture is freedom', he has written. 'I believe this to be a highly important labour because of its formative value for collective cultural growth, without which our revolutions would leave the world as it is'.[22] And this is Munari's profound message, expressed as usual in clear and simple words; he is an artist who is still committed today — like David against Goliath — to challenging the mental and visual conventions and habits of Western man. 'It is merely a question of changing society', says Munari, 'I know that it will take years, but if somebody doesn't start...'[23]

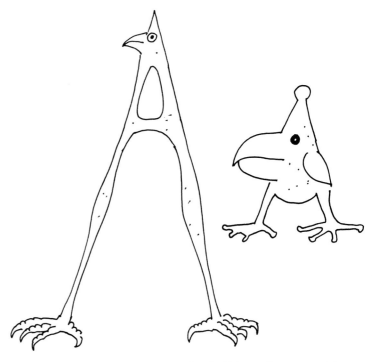

A is for bird, pencil on paper, 1960.

Appearance of our ancestors, marking pens on card, 1970.

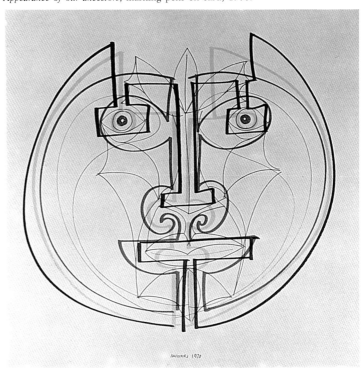

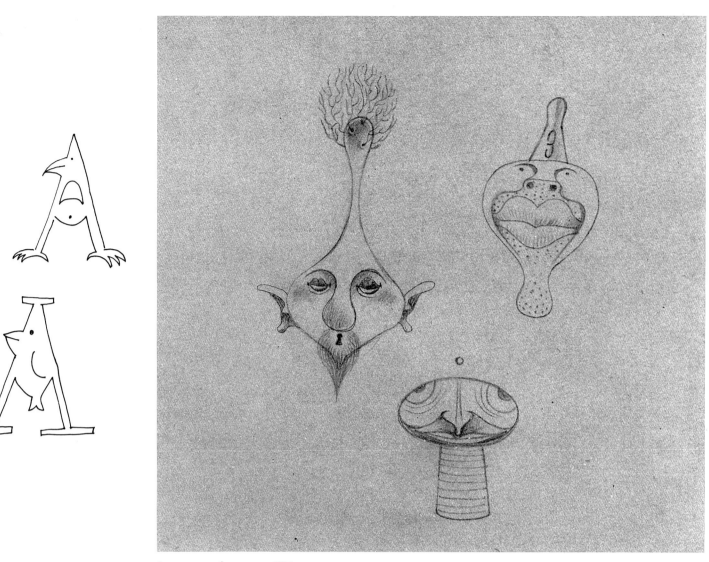

Cartoons, pencil on paper, 1930.

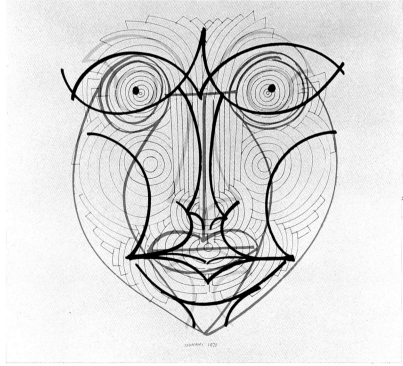

A number of frames from *Scacco matto*, a film investigating cinematographic language, shot at Monte Olimpino by Munari and Marcello Piccardo. A trivial take of a few seconds in length was repeated for 5 minutes, with continual variations of colour, structure and luminosity, using the technical possibilities of development and printing.

Polariscope,
1965. Motorised object using polarised light, with continually changing colours.

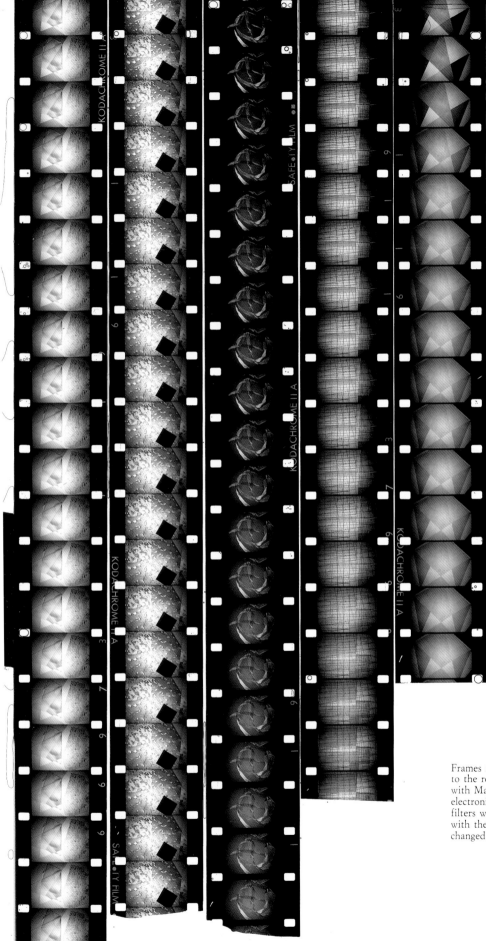

Munari with students of the school
of design in Milan.

121

Frames from the film *I colori della luce* (1963). A sequel
to the researches into polarised light, the film was made
with Marcello Piccardo and its soundtrack was a piece of
electronic music composed by Luciano Berio. Polarising
filters were used to obtain the break-up of white light,
with the resulting colours recorded as they continually
changed.

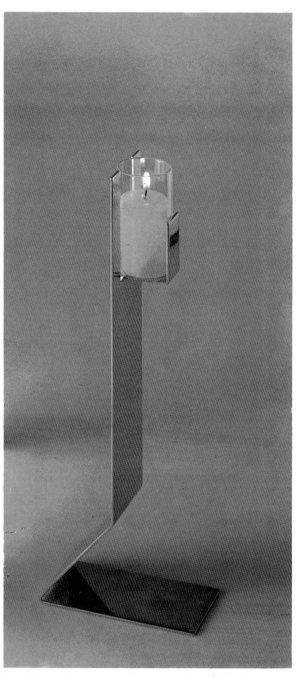

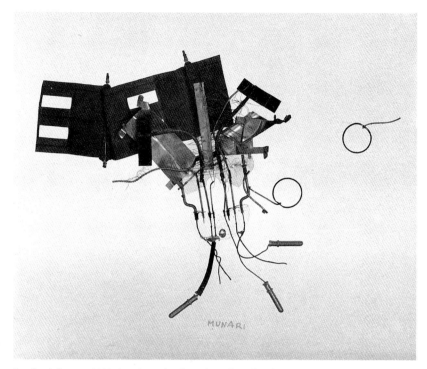

Fossils of the year 2000, interiors of radio valves shaped and
set in transparent polyester resin, 1959.

Candlestick, stainless steel and pyrex, manufactured by Danese, 1973.

Tetracone, motor-driven kinetic multiple, 1965.

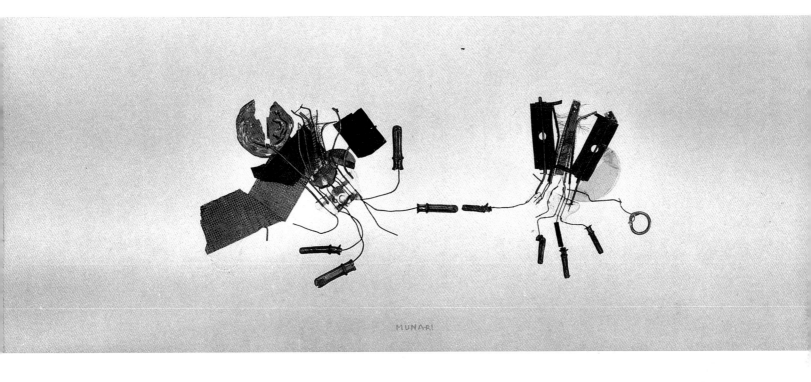

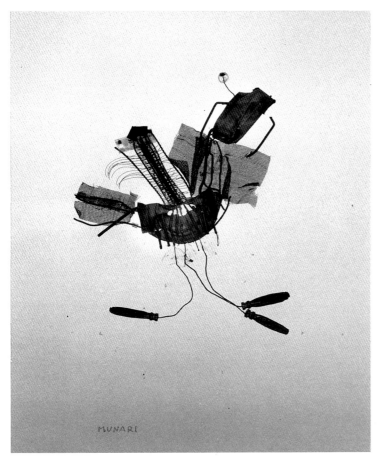

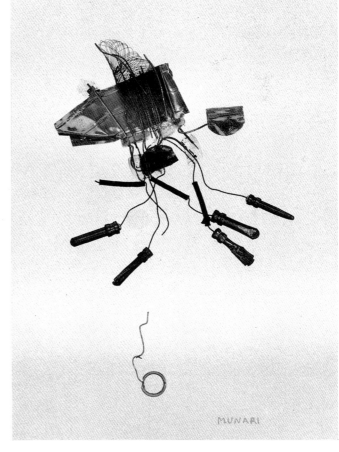

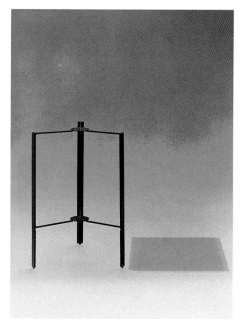  

Dattilo lamp, plastic and enamelled metal, manufactured by Danese, 1978.

Indecipherable script of an unknown people,
1974, Galleria Sincron, Brescia.

Campari poster, collage of Campari logotypes altered
by a colour photocopier.

Munari has written a great deal: educational books,
devoted to design; presentations for his own exhibitions
or objects; articles for magazines and newspapers; books
that are at once bizarre, humorous and polemical. His
first book, *Le macchine di Munari*, dates from 1940 and is
full of Surrealistic vim, but always turned in a 'logical'
direction, however absurd: for example, the idea of
printing a newspaper on rubber 'for the use of the short-
sighted who, without having to look for their glasses,
would be able with a slight effort to stretch the paper to
the right size'. In this one hears an echo of Alphonse
Allais or Campanile.

Cubist bicycle, collage, 1940.

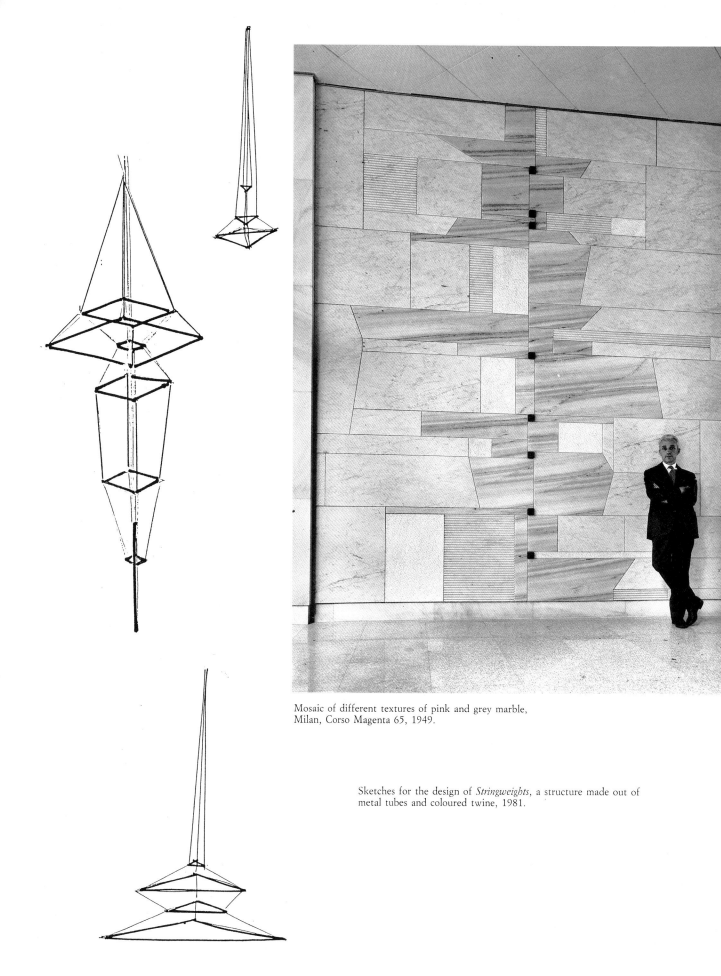

Mosaic of different textures of pink and grey marble,
Milan, Corso Magenta 65, 1949.

Sketches for the design of *Stringweights*, a structure made out of
metal tubes and coloured twine, 1981.

127

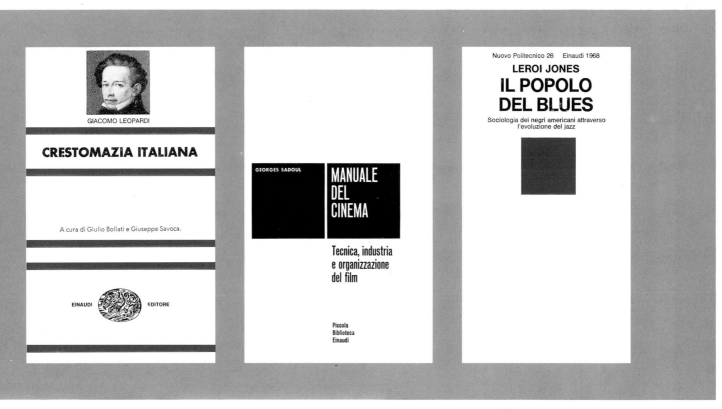

Placard for bookshop and three covers
for Einaudi series that are still in print.

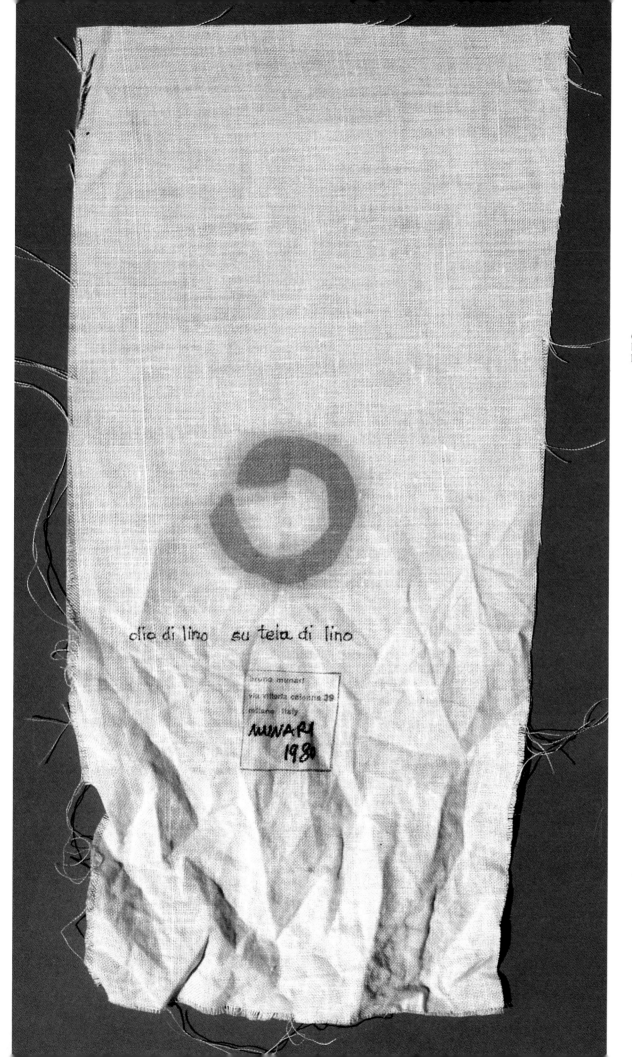

olio di lino su tela di lino

bruno munari
via vittoria colonna 39
milano Italy
MUNARI
1980

Oil on canvas,
linseed oil on
linen, 1980.

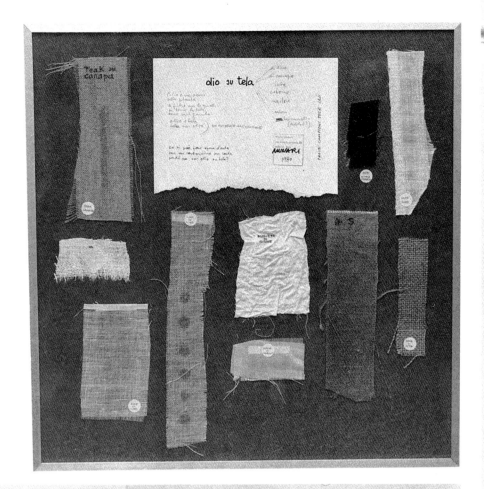

Oil on canvas, examples of fabrics and oils made from different plants, 1980-1986.

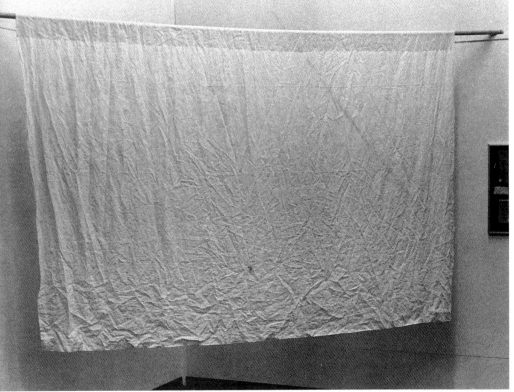

Visual connections between elements of Peano's curve, printing and Indian ink, 1974.

'In order to demonstrate that curved lines without tangents can exist, the famous mathematician Giuseppe Peano (1858-1932) devised a curved line, resembling the thread that forms a mesh, but so dense as to completely fill the area of a square. The result was a black square.

The famous line is visible in the boundaries between zones of colour in this composition of mine.

My proposal, absolutely irrelevant to mathematical speculation, but a curious one from the aesthetic angle, consists in placing particular colours in the zones delimited by the line.

Confronted by this proposal the observer is led to imagine what might be the colour of the square surface when the curve, growing smaller and multiplying *ad infinitum*, will have filled it almost entirely.

It is not necessary to think about it continually, once in a while is enough.'

Bruno Munari, 1974

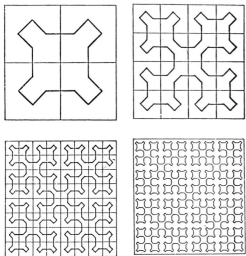

The outline that defines Peano's curve.

Colours in Peano's curve, acrylic on canvas, 1974.

131

Colours in Peano's curve, acrylic on canvas, 1975.

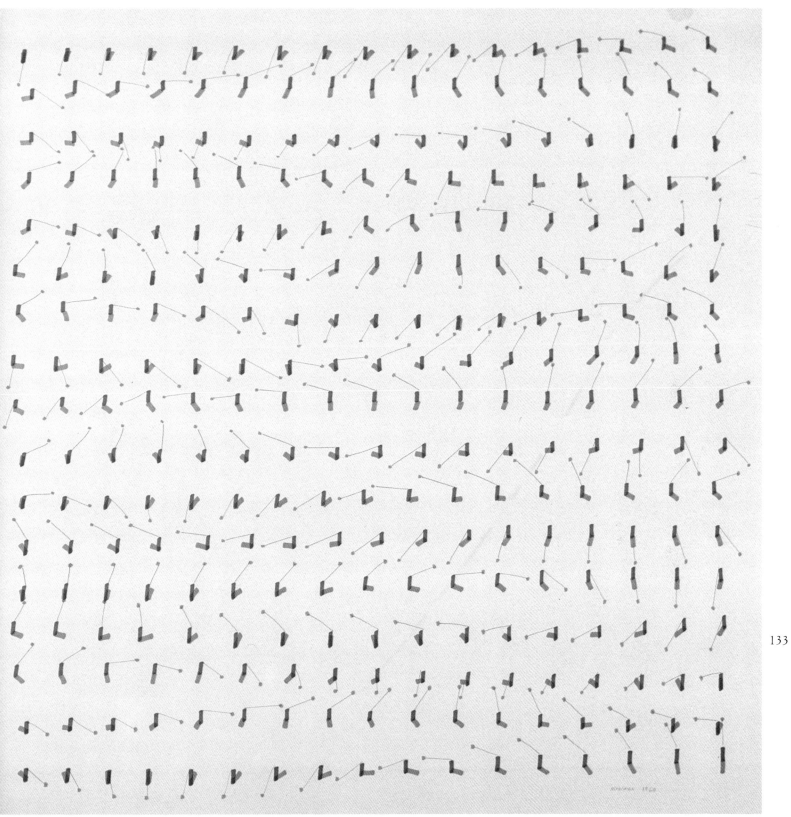

133

Study for the programming of forms in movement, coloured pencils on paper, 1960.

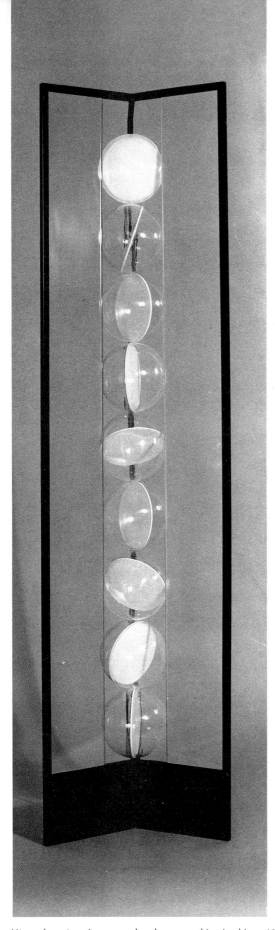

Nine spheres in column, metal and perspex, kinetic object, 1963.

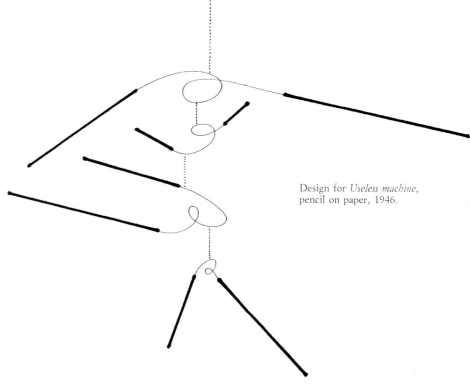

Design for *Useless machine*, pencil on paper, 1946.

   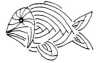

50 examples of *X hour*, made by Danese, 1945-1963.

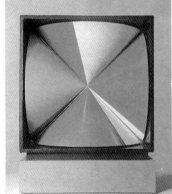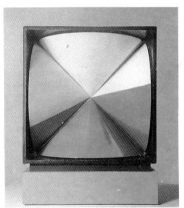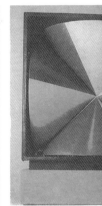

Variations of a *Tetracone*.

135

In 1962 the first exhibition of programmed art was held in Milan, under the auspices of Olivetti. The exhibition was organised by Munari, with a theoretical contribution from Umberto Eco. Born in the era of New Dada and Nouveau Réalisme, programmed art was based on experimentation and non-subjectivity, in accordance with a scientific method that took account of technical aspects and psychological data concerning perception. In contrast to other forms of kinetic art, programmed art was not concerned with composition, but with rigorous programming of materials, forms and kinetic combinations, in order to establish with precision the message to be communicated and choice of means of expression, free from aesthetic or stylistic preconceptions.

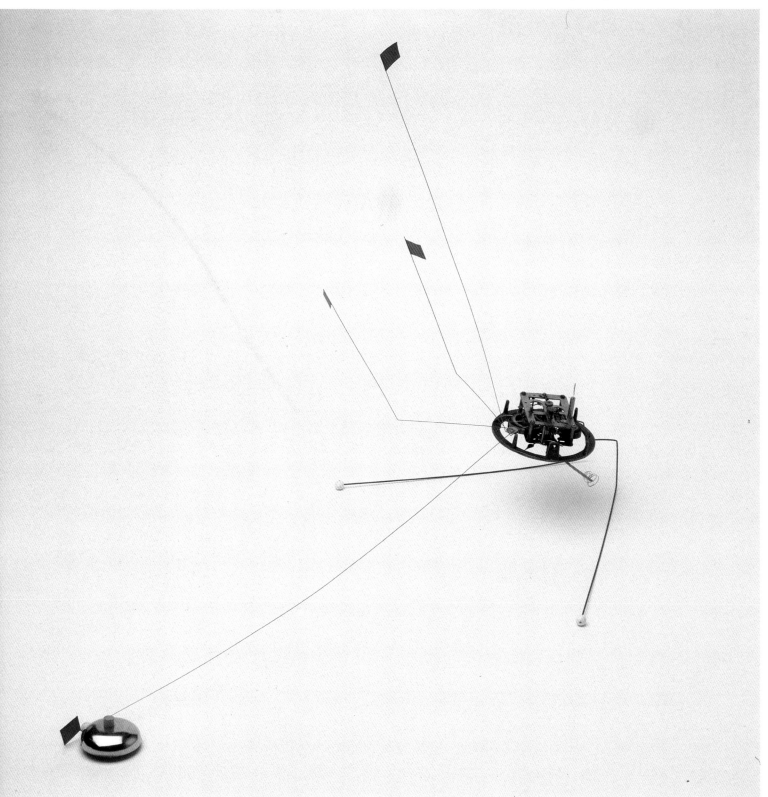

Arhythmic machine, metal and plastic materials, 1950-1980.

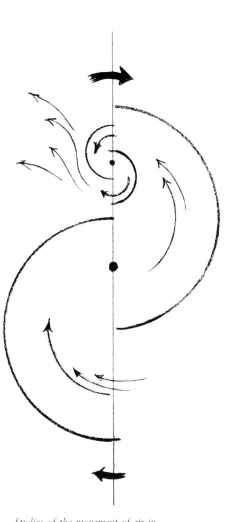

Studies of the movement of air in a rotating form, pencil on paper, 1969.

Making the air visible, using strips of paper as a learning device, 1969.

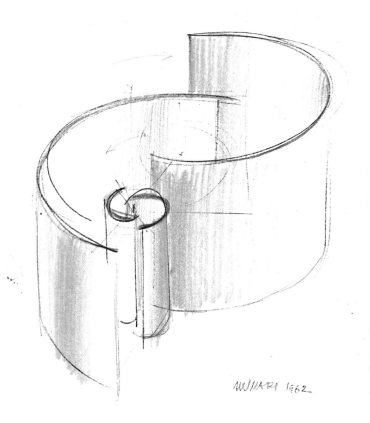

To get a clear idea of Munari's creativity it is necessary to refer to the concept of art current among the ancient Greeks (*techne*, skilful know-how) and to the homologous Japanese concept (*asobi*, play for the pleasure of playing). Munari sets out to balance technique (and technology) with play, for instance in educational ventures like 'Making the air visible', an action-cum-demonstration from 1969.

A number of 'shapes revealing the air' were thrown from the top of a tower: simple sheets of paper, folded in various ways, that followed different trajectories in their fall, according to their shapes and the movement of the air. To comprehend this subtle device fully, it is necessary to bear in mind a line from a Zen poem: 'The trees reveal the bodily form of the wind'.

137

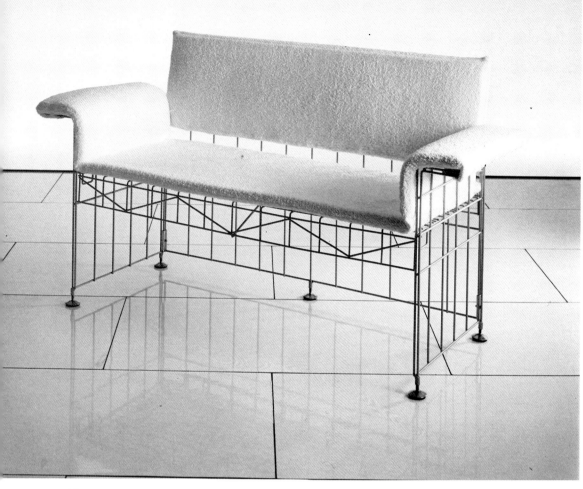

Divanetta, divan for outdoor use with steel structure. Robots, 1986. Munari describes it as follows:
'It has a subtle and harmonious structure
it is slender robust and comfortable
it prefers to stay in the garden
or on the terrace amidst plants and flowers
during transport it folds up
but does not like to stay closed
in a box of 130 × 85 × 23 centimetres
as it feels useless
rather it likes to be covered
with furs tapestries cushions
or rare and unusual or curious materials
it accepts even ribbons and fringes
according to the taste of its owner
Naked it is very beautiful.'

Notes

From childhood to the 1930s

1. In the catalogue *Le persone che hanno fatto grande Milano. Bruno Munari*, no. 26, Sale dell'Alemagna, Milan, 1983, p. 3.
2. A. Branzi, *Il gioco del fare. Intervista con Bruno Munari*. in *Modo*, nos. 71-72, August-September 1984, p. 40.
3. B. Munari, *Arte come mestiere*, Laterza 1966, p. 251.
4. In A. Branzi, *op. cit.*, p. 41.
5. *Ibid.*, p. 41.
6. E. Crispolti, 'Svolgimenti del futurismo', in the catalogue of the exhibition *Gli Anni Trenta*, Mazzotta 1982, p. 176.
7. G. Balla and F. Depero, *Ricostruzione Futurista dell'Universo*, Milan, March 1915.
8. E. Crispolti, *op. cit.*, p. 176.
9. 'Artecrazia', supplement to *Futurismo*, 1-15 July 1932, p. 42.
10. In 'Sant'Elia', supplement to *Futurismo*, March 1, 1934, p. 6.
11. P. Mondrian, *Tutti gli scritti*, Feltrinelli 1975, p. 269.
12. B. Munari, *op. cit.*, p. 10.
13. Quoted in A. Schwarz, *La sposa messa a nudo in Marcel Duchamp*, Einaudi 1974, p. 152.
14. P. Fossati, in B. Munari, *Codice Ovvio*, Einaudi 1971, p. 133.

Graphics, theatre, painting, writing and other activities

1. Quoted in C.A. Quintavalle, *Pubblicità. Modello, sistema, storia*, Feltrinelli 1977, p. 55.
2. *Ibid.*, p. 55.
3. In L. Scrivo, *Sintesi del futurismo*, Bulzoni 1968, p. 199.
4. Presentation *Quattro atti unici Nô*, Milan, Teatro degli Omenoni, 1962, p. 7.
5. In P. Fossati, *La realtà attrezzata*, Einaudi 1977, p. 231.

6. A. Marasco, in *Origini*, May-June 1943, p. 6.
7. *Ibid.*, p. 6.
8. L. Pralavorio, 'Delle Macchine Inutili e di altro', in *Cronaca Prealpina*, May 28, 1934 (now in the catalogue *Bruno Munari*, Parma, 1979).
9. B. Munari, 'Manifesto del Macchinismo' (1938), in *Arte Concreta* no. 10, pub. by Arte Concreta 1952 (now in the catalogue *Bruno Munari*, *op. cit.*).
10. B. Munari, *Codice ovvio, op. cit.*, p. 50.
11. F. Menna, 'Munari o la coincidenza degli opposti', in *La botte e il violino*, no. 3, 1966 (now in catalogue *Bruno Munari*, *op. cit.*).
12. B. Munari, *Arte come mestiere, op. cit.*, p. 232.
13. F. Menna, *op. cit.*
14. B. Munari, *op. cit.*, p. 169.
15. B. Munari, *Le macchine di Munari*, Einaudi 1942, p. 9.
16. B. Munari, *Artista e designer*, Laterza 1971, p. 84.
17. B. Munari, *Arte come mestiere, op. cit.*, p. 46.

Art as profession

1. A. Tofanelli, in the catalogue *Le persone...*, *op. cit.*, p. 12.
2. B. Munari, in the catalogue *Arte Concreta*, no. 10, 1952 (now in the catalogue *Bruno Munari*, *op. cit.*).
3. B. Munari, 'L'arte è un mestiere', in *AZ*, no. 1, January 1950, p. 1.
4. B. Munari, *Design e comunicazione visiva*, Laterza 1974, p. 50.
5. B. Munari, *Codice ovvio, op. cit.*, p. 76.
6. B. Munari, *Design...*, *op. cit.*, p. 75.
7. B. Munari, *Codice ovvio, op. cit.*, p. 116.
8. *Ibid.*, p. 5.
9. B. Munari, *Arte come mestiere, op. cit.*, pp. 136-138.

10. G.C. Argan, in the catalogue, *Bruno Munari*, *op. cit.*, p. 11.
11. B. Munari, *Codice ovvio, op. cit.*, p. 97.
12. *Ibid.*, p. 89.
13. P. Klee, *Teoria della forma e della figurazione*, Feltrinelli 1969, p. 453.

Towards an art for everyone

1. B. Munari, *Da cosa nasce cosa*, Laterza 1981, p. 108.
2. *Ibid.*, p. 297.
3. *Ibid.*, p. 379.
4. P. Klee, *op. cit.*, p. 168.
5. B. Munari, *Fantasia*, Laterza 1977, p. 143.
6. P. Klee, *op. cit.*, p. 71.
7. *Ibid.*, p. 63.
8. *Ibid.*, p. 80.
9. B. Munari, *Arte come mestiere, op. cit.*, p. 21.
10. P. Klee, *op. cit.*, p. 71.
11. B. Munari, *Codice ovvio, op. cit.*, p. 113.
12. U. Eco, *Trattato di semiotica generale*, Bompiani 1975, p. 242.
13. B. Munari, *Codice ovvio, op. cit.*, p. 113.
14. *Ibid.*, p. 97.
15. 'Libri per bambini. Intervista a B.M.', in *N.A.C.*, no. 67, 1971, p. 6.
16. In the catalogue *Bruno Munari*, *op. cit.*, p. 19.
17. *Ibid.*, p. 51.
18. In 'Libri per bambini...', *op. cit.*, p. 6.
19. B. Munari, *Da cosa nasce cosa, op. cit.*, p. 228.
20. Michel Seuphor, *Bonjour Munari*, 1961 (now in the catalogue *Bruno Munari*, *op. cit.*).
21. Shuzo Takiguchi, Presentation for Bruno Munari's one-man show, Tokyo 1965 (now in the catalogue *Bruno Munari*, *op. cit.*).
22. In the catalogue *Bruno Munari*, *op. cit.*, p. 51.
23. In A. Branzi, *op. cit.*, p. 43.

Bibliography

Writings on Bruno Munari

Le onoranze a Umberto Boccioni. L'omaggio degli artisti futuristi, Milan 1932 (now in the catalogue *Bruno Munari*, Parma 1979).
M. Ferrigni, *La pubblicità di una grande casa*, Milan 1937.
A. de Angelis, *Scenografie di ieri e di oggi*, Rome 1938.
T. d'Albisola, *La ceramica futurista*, Savona 1939.
S. Quasimodo, presentation of Munari's exhibition *Oggetti metafisici*, Milan 1940.
U. Nebbia, *Pittura del Novecento*, Milan 1946.
G. Dorfles, Presentation of Munari's exhibition *Macchine inutili e dipinti*, Milan 1949 (now in the catalogue *Bruno Munari*, Parma 1979).
A. Mondadori, presentation of Munari's exhibition *Libri illeggibili*, Milan 1950 (now in the catalogue *Il Movimento Arte Concreta 1948-1958*, Monza 1984).
P. Hulten, Presentation of Munari's exhibition *Macchine aritmiche*, Stockholm, Museum of Modern Art, 1951.
T. Sauvage, *Pittura italiana del dopoguerra*, Milan 1957.
Gec (E. Gianeri), *Storia del cartone animato*, Milan 1960.
C. Belloli, M. Callewaert, presentation of the exhibition *Bruno Munari*, Antwerp (Belgium), Centruum voor hedendaagse Kunstuitingen, 1960.
M. Seuphor, *Bonjour Munari*, Milan 1961 (now in the catalogue *Bruno Munari*, Parma 1979).
G. Dorfles, *Ultime tendenze dell'arte oggi*, Milan 1961.
'Bruno Munari', in *Who's Who in Graphic Art*, Zurich 1962.
U. Eco, 'La forma del disordine', in *Almanacco Bompiani*, Milan 1962 (now in the catalogue *Bruno Munari*, Parma 1979).
G. Dorfles, *Il disegno industriale e la sua estetica*, Bologna 1963.
C. Manzoni, *Gli anni verdi del Bertoldo*, Milan 1964.
G. Ballo, *La linea dell'arte italiana*, Rome 1964.
S. Takiguchi, presentation of the exhibition *Bruno Munari* Tokyo 1965 (now in the catalogue Bruno Munari, Parma 1979).
F. Menna, 'Bruno Munari', in the catalogue of the XXXIII Triennale, Venice 1966.
M. Fagiolo dell'Arco, *Rapporto '60*, Rome 1966.
F. Popper, *Naissance de l'art cinétique*, Paris 1967.
C.L. Ragghianti, in the exhibition catalogue *Arte moderna in Italia 1915-1935*, Florence 1967.
L. Caramel, presentation of Munari's exhibition *Original xerographs*, Como 1969.
L. Caramel, in the exhibition catalogue *Aspetti del primo astrattismo italiano 1930-1940*, Monza 1969.
E. Crispolti, *Il mito della macchina e altri temi del futurismo*, Trapani 1969.
G.C. Argan, *L'arte moderna 1770-1970*, Florence 1970.
B. Zevi, *Cronache d'architettura*, Bari 1970.
P. Fossati, presentation of Munari's exhibition *Munari 1971*, Milan 1971.
I. Tomassoni, *Arte dopo il 1945. Italia*, Bologna 1971.
P. Fossati, *Il design in Italia 1945-1972*, Turin 1972.
C. Belloli, presentation of the exhibition *Bruno Munari: dalle Macchine inutili alle nuove ludopedagogie della comunicazione visiva*, Milan 1978.
C. Belli, *Lettera sulla nascita dell'astrattismo italiano*, Milan 1978.

P. Serra Zanetti, 'Ricerche ottiche visive e arte cinetico-programmata', in *L'arte in Italia nel secondo dopoguerra*, Bologna 1979.
E. Crispolti, in the exhibition catalogue *Ricostruzione futurista dell'universo*, Turin 1980.
P. Fossati, *Il Movimento Arte Concreta*, Turin 1980.
G. Anzani, L. Caramel, *Scultura moderna in Lombardia*, Milan 1981.
A. Tanchis, *L'arte anomala di Bruno Munari*, Bari 1981.
L. Caramel, 'Gli astratti', in the exhibition catalogue *Gli Anni Trenta*, Milan 1982.
E. Crispolti, 'Svolgimenti del futurismo', in the exhibition catalogue *Gli Anni Trenta*, Milan 1982.
M. Pigozzi, 'La grafica industriale nel sistema della comunicazione', in the exhibition catalogue *Gli Anni Trenta*, Milan 1982.
E. Crispolti, in the exhibition catalogue *La ceramica futurista da Balla a Tullio d'Albisola*, Albissola 1982.
M. Prazzi, A. Tofanelli, G. Tarozzi, in the exhibition catalogue *Le persone che hanno fatto grande Milano*, Milan 1983.
G. Anzani, L. Caramel, *Pittura moderna in Lombardia*, Milan 1983.
L. Caramel, in the exhibition catalogue *Il Movimento Arte Concreta 1948-1958*, Monza 1984.
Various authors, exhibition catalogue *Bruno Munari*, Tokyo 1985.
C. Vivaldi, presentation of the exhibition *Come nasce un libro?*, Rome 1985.
Various authors, *Futurismo e futurismi*, Milan 1986.
M. Meneguzzo, exhibition catalogue *Bruno Munari*, Milan 1986.

Books designed, written and illustrated by Bruno Munari

1940
Almanacco Dada (unpublished).
1942
Le macchine di Munari.
1944
Fotocronache (reprint of a limited edition in 1980).
1945
Disegni astratti.
I libri Munari (published in English as *Jimmy Has Lost His Cap*, *Animals For Sales*, *The Birthday Present*, *The Elephant Wish*, *Tic, Tac and Toc*, *Who's There?*, *Open the Door*, by The World Publishing Company, New York 1957).
1947
Che cos'è il termometro.
Che cos'è l'orologio.
1950
Libri illeggibili (handmade, limited edition).
1953
Libro illeggibile bianco e rosso.
1958
Le forchette di Munari.
1959
Le forchette di Munari.
1960
Alfabetiere.
ABC and *Munari's Zoo*, The World Publishing Company, New York (reprint 1982).
1961
Teoremi sull'arte.

1963
Good design.
Supplemento al dizionario italiano.
1964
La scoperta del cerchio.
L'idea è nel filo.
1965
Libro illeggibile bianco e nero (published in Japan).
1966
Libro illeggibile trasparente.
Arte come mestiere (published in English as *Design as Art*, Penguin, 1971).
1967
Libro illeggibile N.Y. 1, Museum of Modern Art, New York.
1968
Design e comunicazione visiva.
Nella nebbia di Milano.
Un fiore con amore.
1970
Xerografie.
1971
Da lontano era un'isola.
Artista e designer.
Codice ovvio.
1972
Xerografie originali.
Cappuccetto verde.
Cappuccetto giallo.
1973
Rose nell'insalata.
1976
La scoperta del triangolo.
1977
Fantasia.
Xerografie originali.
1978
La scoperta del quadrato.
Guida ai lavori in legno (with R. Donzelli and P. Polato).
1979
Disegnare il sole.
1980
Disegnare un albero.
1981
Da cosa nasce cosa.

Books illustrated by Bruno Munari

1929
Aquilotto implume, by Toscano.
1933
L'anguria lirica (with Diulgheroff), by Tullio d'Albisola.
Il cantastorie di Campari.
1937
Poema del vestito di latte, by F.T. Marinetti.
1962
Il pianeta degli alberi di Natale, by G. Rodari.
1966
La torta in cielo, by G. Rodari.
1972
A-uli'-ule', by N. Orengo.
1975
Favole al telefono, by G. Rodari.

Series of books directed by Bruno Munari
Tantibambini, Einaudi.
Quaderni del design, Zanichelli.
Giocare con l'arte, Zanichelli.
Disegnare Colorare Costruire, Zanichelli.

Arrangement of dwelling-blocks in a park of trees drawn by children.

Chronology of works

1927
Paintings: *Constructing*.
Drawings on paper: *Portrait of Russolo*,
Dynamism of motorcyclist.
1928
Paintings: *Radiovision*.
Futurist ceramics: *Imaginary animals*.
1929
Paintings and drawings.
Illustrates Marinetti's *Il suggeritore nudo*.
Advertising cartoon films.
Starts to contribute, as an illustrator, to *Grandi
firme*, *Lidel*, *Settebello*, *Commedia*, *Il Corriere dei
Piccoli*.
1930
Paintings: *Self-portrait*, *Hand*.
Cover for *Anime Sceneggiate* by P. Masnata.
Illustrations for *Il Giovedì*.
Aerial machine.
1931
Paintings: *Pause in the air*.
Illustrates Marinetti's *Il Teatro totale delle masse*.
1932
Works employing different materials: *Adventure
on pink sky*, *Radioscopy of the modern man*,
Thicknesses of atmosphere.
Covers and illustrations for *La Natura*.
1933
Useless machines (in wood, cotton and drawing
paper)
Subway decoration of station for airport (at the
fifth Triennial Exhibition in Milan)
Illustrates, with Diulgheroff, *L'anguria lirica*,
litho plate/sheet by Tullio d'Albisola; *Il
cantastorie di Campari* (5th series).
Industrial design for fabrics.
1934
Paintings: *At the limits of painting*, *Machines in
the wood*, *Beach*.
Mural at the Aeronautics Show in Milan.
Tactile table.
1935
Abstract paintings: *The frame too* (I, II, III).
Set designs for *Danza sui trampoli* and *Acrobati
musicali in gabbia*.
Palette of typographical possibilities.
Pages up, with Ricas, issue no. 5 of *L'Ufficio
Moderno*.
1936
Set design for act III of *Joshitomo*, and six
masks, at the sixth Triennial Exhibition.
Illustrations for *Il Bertoldo*.
1937
Abstract paintings: *A blue point*.
Pages up and illustrates *Il poema del vestito di
latte*, by Marinetti.
Illustrations and cover for *La Lettura*.
1938
Abstract and surrealistic drawings.
Contributes to *Il Milione*.
1939
Directs the art department of *Tempo*.
1940
Metaphysical objects.
Collages and *photomontages*.
Dada almanac.
Drawings (*Lines under tension*).
Sensitivity.
Graphic fantasies at the seventh Triennial
Exhibition.
1941
Temperas and abstract drawings.

1943
Drawings (*Lines under tension*)
Abstract tempera.
1944
Abstract paintings.
1945
Abstract paintings.
Drawings (*Leaves*).
Metaphysical object.
Message in a bottle.
First *Children's books*.
X hour.
1946
Metaphysical objects
1947
Useless machines (in transparent plastic).
Archipelago (abstract tempera).
Drawings for *Stringweights*.
1948
Concave convexes.
Abstract tempera: *Homage to Arp*.
Collages and *Photomontages*.
1949
First *Unreadable books*.
1950
Negative positives.
Stringweights.
Bugle of peace.
Abstract temperas: *32 abstract designs*.
1951
Arhythmic machines.
1952
Birobotanics, sketches with ball-point pen.
Fountain for the Biennial Exhibition in Venice.
Paintings: *Sequences*.
1953
Direct projections.
1954
*Toys that can be manipulated into different
positions* (Compasso d'Oro).
Advertising spectacles made from cardboard, for
Imago dp.
1956
Theoretical reconstructions of imaginary objects.
Cerchio fountain.
Desk set, Danese.
Ice-bucket for thermos, for Meo.
1957
Cubic ashtray, Danese.
Projections with polarised light.
1958
Travelling sculptures.
Munari's forks.
Bali lamp, Danese.
Calendar, Lucini.
1959
Fossils of the year 2000
Prismatic lamp, Danese.
Nickel-silver bowl, Danese.
Painting: *Cybernetic perturbation*.
1961
Continuous structures, Danese.
Fountain for the Fiera di Milano.
Stromboli candlesticks, Danese.
Capri lamp, Danese.
Galapagos picture-frame, Danese.
Moluccas and *Hainain stamps for correspondence*,
Danese.
1962
Nine spheres in column, kinetic multiple.
Set-design for '4 one-act dramas from the Nô
Theatre'.

1963
Sets up, with Piccardo, the Experimental
Cinematographic Centre in Monte Olimpino.
Experimental films: *I colori della luce*, *Inox*,
Moire, *Tempo nel tempo*.
Production of *X hour*, 'the first mass-produced
kinetic object' (Popper).
1964
Falkland tubular lamp, Danese.
Favignana show-case, Danese.
1965
Tetracone.
5-drop fountain.
Original xerographs.
Campari poster.
Alicudi food-warmer, Danese.
1966
Polariscope.
Appearance of our ancestors.
Structure for exhibitions, Danese.
1968
Flexy, Danese.
Munari and *No Non Nein Ne* posters.
1969
Aria, performance at the 'Campo Urbano' event,
Como.
1970
Let's look each other in the eye.
Rubber picture-frame, Danese.
1971
Abitacolo, Robots.
Lipari ashtray, Danese.
1972
Structures. Educational game, Danese (with G.
Belgrano).
Biplano trolley, Robots.
1973
Roses in the salad.
Panarea candlestick, Danese.
Labirinto (Maze), *Più e meno* (More and less),
Carte da gioco (playing cards), educational games
for Danese (with G. Belgrano).
Metti le foglie - Alberi (Place the leaves - Trees),
educational game for Danese.
Bookcase, Robots.
1974
Chromatic proposals for Peano's curve.
Vademecum carrying structure, Robots.
1976
Indecipherable scripts of unknown peoples.
Tactile message for a sightless little girl.
Giocare con l'arte (Playing with art), workshop
for the development of creativity in children
staged at the Museo di Brera, then in Faenza,
Barcelona, Geneva and Tokyo.
1977
Immagini della realtà (Images of reality),
educational game for Danese (with G. Belgrano).
*Visualisation of harmonic structures in the visual
work of art*, for the Museo di Brera.
1978
Dattilo lamp, Danese.
1979
Pre-books.
1980
Oil on canvas.
Patchwork.
1981
Stringweights.
1985
The Divanetta, Robots.
Carpet, Sisal.
Textiles for interior decoration, Assia.
1986
Posters for Campari.

Exhibitions by Bruno Munari

One-man shows

1933
Galleria delle Tre Arti, Milan.
1940
Metaphysical objects, Galleria del Milione, Milan.
1944
Abstract paintings, Galleria Ciliberti, Milan.
1946
Galleria Bergamini, Milan.
1948
Galleria Borromini, Milan; *Artists' toys*, Galleria dell'Annunciata, Milan; Sale di Fede Cheti, Milan.
1949
Munari's aerial plastics, Galleria del Cavallino, Venice; *Useless machines and paintings*, Libreria Salto, Milan.
1950
Unreadable books, Libreria Salto, Milan.
1951
Arythmic machines, Museum of Modern Art, Stockholm.
Found objects, Galleria dell'Annunciata, Milan.
1952
Negative positives, Galleria Bergamini, Milan.
1953
Unreadable books, Italian Book and Craft, New York.
Direct projections, Studio B24, Milan.
1954
Direct projections, Museum of Modern Art, New York; Studio Lionni, New York.
1955
Direct projections, Galleria del Fiore, Milan; Galleria Nazionale d'Arte Moderna, Rome; Galleria Numero, Florence.
1956
Theoretical reconstructions of imaginary objects, Galleria San Babila, Milan; *Projections with polarised light*; Studio B24, Milan (and contemporaneously in Rome, Tokyo, New York, Stockholm, Antwerp, Zurich and Amsterdam).
1957
Direct projections, Gallery Christofle, Paris.
1958
Travelling sculptures, Galleria Montenapoleone, Milan.
1960
Bruno Munari, Centruum voor hedendaagse Kunstuitingen, Antwerp (Belgium).
1961
Continuous structures, Danese, Milan; *Projection with polarised light*, Teatro Ruzante, Padua.
1964
Gallery Object, Zurich.
1965
Bruno Munari, Isetan, Tokyo.
1966
Howard Wise Gallery, New York, Galleria dell'Obelisco, Rome; Oneman show at the 33rd Biennial Exhibition in Venice, Galleria Modern Art, Naples.
1967
Works in series from 1958 to the present day, Galleria Vismara, Milan, *Xerographs*, Danese, Milan.
1968
Original xerographs, Serendipity 54, Rome; Galleria La Colonna, Como; Galleria Sincron, Brescia; Allgemeine Gewerbeschule, Basle; *Creativity right away*, Galleria Blu, Milan; Galleria L'Incontro, Ostiglia; Galleria Sincron, Brescia; Gallery Cadaques, Cadaques; Galleria Uxa, Novara; Galleria A, Parma.

1970
Appearance of our ancestors, Danese, Milan.
1976
Indecipherable scripts of unknown peoples, Galleria Mercato del Sale, Milan; Galleria del Portello, Genoa.
1977
Galleria Sincron, Brescia.
1978
Galleria arte struktura, Milan; Galleria 8 + 1, Mestre; Galleria del Portello, Genoa; Galleria Studio F22, Palazzolo sull'Oglio.
1980
Oil on canvas, Galleria Sincron, Brescia; Galleria Apollinaire, Milan; Danese, Milan.
1981
Servizi culturali di Olivetti, Ivrea; Galleria Sincron, Brescia; Danese, Milan.
1982
Centro culturale Magazzino dei fiori, Genoa; Studio AM, Rome.
1983
Galleria Sincron, Brescia.
1984
Studio d'arte, Trieste; Museo di Arte Moderno Fundaciòn Soto, Ciudad Bolivar; Galerìa Municipal, Puerto la Cruz; Centro de Bellas Artes, Maracaibo; Ateneo de Valencia, Valencia; Casa de la Cultura, Maracay; Museo de Barquisimeto, Barquisimeto; Museo de los Niños y Museo de Bellas Artes, Caracas.
1985
'The house today' tactile space, Cesena; Galleria Corraini, Mantua; total realisation of all children's workshops, Kodomo no shiro, Tokyo.
1986
One-man show at the 43rd Biennial Exhibition in Venice; anthological/retrospective exhibition *Bruno Munari*, Palazzo Reale, Milan.

Group exhibitions

1927
Exhibition of 34 Futurist painters, Galleria Pesaro, Milan.
1928
Exhibition of Futurist, Novecentist and Strapaese Art, Teatro scientifico, Mantua.
1929
33 Futurist painters, Galleria Pesaro, Milan.
1930
17th Biennial Exhibition in Venice; *Peintres futuristes italiens*, Galerie 23, Paris; *Futurist exhibition architect Sant'Elia and 23 Futurist painters*, Galleria Pesaro, Milan.
1931
Futurist exhibition of air-brush painting and set-design, Galleria Pesaro, Milan; *1st Quadrennial Exhibition in Rome*; *Futurist exhibition of painting, sculpture and decorative art*, Palazzo della Permanente, Chiavari.
1932
18th Biennial Exhibition in Venice; *Exhibition of Futurist airbrush painting*, Galleria Pesaro, Milan; *Prampolini et les aeropeintres futuristes italiens*, Galerie de la Renaissance, Paris.
1933
5th Triennial Exhibition in Milan; *Futurist exhibition in homage to Umberto Boccioni*, Galleria Pesaro, Milan; *Exhibition of the rejected national and international road sign*, Galleria del Milione, Milan.

1934
Aeronautics Show, Milan; *Selection of twenty-five-year-old Futurists*, Galleria Tre Arti, Milan; *Les aeropeintres futuristes italiens*, Nice, Hotel Negresco.
1935
2nd Quadrennial Exhibition in Rome.
1936
6th Triennial Exhibition in Milan; *Exhibition of graphic art*, Galleria del Milione, Milan.
1940
7th Triennial Exhibition in Milan.
1947
International exhibition of concrete art, Palazzo Reale, Milan.
1949
Circolo di Cultura, Lugano.
1950
Abstract and concrete art in Italy, Galleria Nazionale d'Arte Moderna, Rome.
1951
Galleria Bergamini, Milan; First exhibition of industrial arts and aesthetics, 30th Milan Trade Fair; *The artists of the MAC*, Galleria Bompiani, Milan.
1953
MAC, Ministry of Education, Santiago, Chile; Amigos del Arte, Santa Fè; Galleria Viale Roma, Bergamo.
1955
Two graphic designers, Museum of Modern Art, New York.
1960
From nature to art, Palazzo Grassi, Venice.
1962
Programmed art, Olivetti, Milan.
1967
Modern art in Italy 1915-1935, Palazzo Strozzi, Florence.
1968
Fifteen masters of abstractionism, Galleria Vismara, Milan.
1969
Aspects of early Italian abstractionism 1930-1940, Galleria Civica d'Arte Moderna, Monza.
1970
Kinetics - International Survey, Hayward Gallery, London.
1971
Italian art, Istituto italiano di cultura, Montevideo.
1973
Suvreme Umietnosti, Zagreb; Studentski Kulturni Center Gallery, Belgrade; Radnicki Universitet Gallery, Novi Sad.
1975
Galleria A, Parma; Museo Progressivo, Livorno; Museo d'Arte Moderna, Bologna.
1980
Patchwork in Italy, Studio Marconi, Milan; *Futurist reconstruction of the universe*, Musei Civici, Turin.
1982
Futurist ceramics from Balla to Tullio d'Albissola, Sale di Villa Gavetti, Albisola superiore; Palazzo delle Esposizioni, Faenza; *The thirties*, Palazzo Reale, Milan.
1984
The Concrete Art Movement 1948-1958, Civica Galleria d'Arte Moderna, Gallarate.
1985
Come nasce un libro?, Palazzo Valentini, Rome.

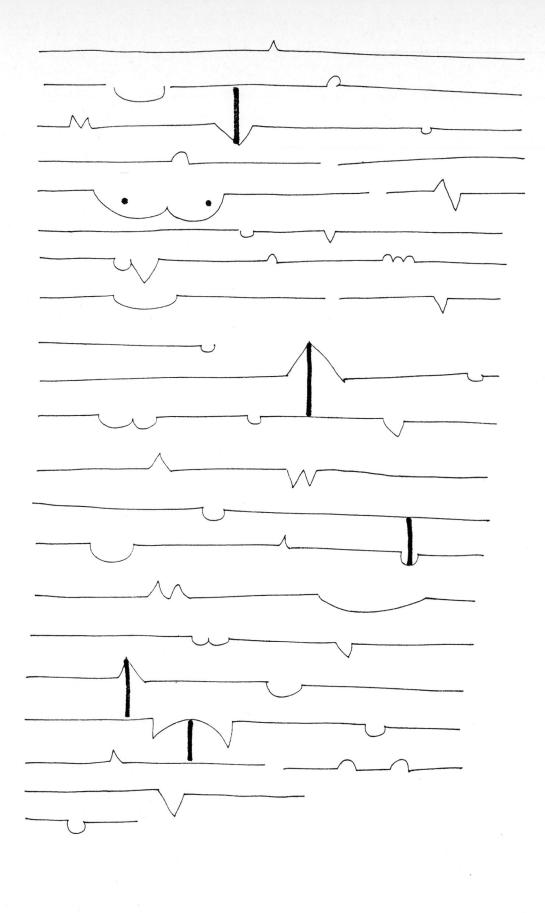